Logic and Islam

Logic and Islam
Part I: Faith issues

Answers to current questions

By
Prof. Dr. Magd Abdel Wahab

Uitgeverij Aspekt

Logic and Islam
© Prof. Dr. Magd Abdel Wahab
© 2019 Aspekt Publishers
Aspekt Publishers | Amersfoortsestraat 27
3769 AD Soesterberg | The Netherlands
info@uitgeverijaspekt.nl | www.uitgeverijaspekt.nl
Coverdesign: Mark Heuveling
Lay-out: Paul Timmerman

ISBN: 978-94-6338-582-4
NUR: 717

Disclaimer – The author and the publisher have made every feasible effort to determine and acquire copyright permissions for material presented in this book. If any right-holders have been overlooked we kindly request them to apply to the publisher.

Content

Preface		7
Words of thanks		11
0	**Introduction**	13
1	**Almighty God (Allah SWT)**	23
	1.1 What is the logic in the existence of Almighty God?	23
	1.2 Is nature god?	30
	1.3 Can life be designed by chance or without a designer?	36
	1.4 Who created Almighty God?	43
	1.5 Why only one god?	46
2	**The creation**	51
	2.1 Why has Almighty God created life and people?	51
	2.2 Why has Almighty God created evil?	61
	2.3 Can science create?	67
3	**The soul**	75
	3.1 What is the difference between the soul and the spirit?	75
	3.2 Does the soul exist?	77
4	**The hereafter**	85
	4.1 What is proof of the hereafter?	85
	4.2 Do paradise and hell exist?	91
	4.3 Will non-Muslims go to paradise or hell?	99
5	**Destiny and freedom of choice**	107
	5.1 Do we choose our deeds or are they written for us?	107

6 The holy Quran — 115
6.1 Has prophet Mohammed PBUH copied the holy Quran from the Bible and the Torah? — 115
6.2 What is the miracle of the holy Quran? — 120
6.3 Has prophet Mohammed PBUH written the holy Quran? — 124
6.4 What is the proof that the holy Quran was revealed by Almighty God? — 127

7 The Islam — 135
7.1 Why Islam as a religion? — 135
7.2 Why was Mohammed PBUH chosen to be prophet? — 139
7.3 Why was prophet Mohammed PBUH the last messenger of Almighty God? — 143
7.4 Is the Tawaf a sort of worshipping stone? — 145

About the author — 151

Preface

Throughout history, a believer did not need logical proof to believe in Almighty God. This is because the spiritual proof was always enough to admit the existence of Almighty God and to submit to Him. Finding Almighty God is not a mathematical equation that needs to be proven. Rather, it is a spiritual feeling due to a call from inside a human being. The relationship between Almighty God and humans is spiritual rather logical.

However, with the advances in science and technology, this spiritual relationship decreases. Nowadays, modern man is looking for logic and scientific answers to many questions relating to Almighty God and religions. In fact, nonbelievers or atheists are not the only ones looking for answers to these types of questions; believers also want to increase their faith and remove doubts from their hearts.

The main objective of this book is to provide logical answers to questions relating to belief in Almighty God, creations and Islam as the last heavenly religion. These questions are grouped under several topics, namely: 1) Almighty God, 2) the creation, 3) the soul, 4) the hereafter, 5) the destiny and freedom in choices, 6) the holy Quran and 7) the Islam.

The main feature of this book is that the author provides logic flowcharts with each presented question relating to the different topics. Each logic flowchart has three phases: a start, a process and an end.

We start the book by logically answering questions relating to the existence of Almighty God. Does Almighty God exist? Can nature create itself? Is nature god? Do life and universe need a designer? Or can they come to existence without a designer? Some people may say we believe only in science, but can science create? Can scientists create a human being in the lab? Can this happen in future? If Almighty God has created everything, then who created Almighty God? Does deoxyribonucleic acid (DNA) prove the existence of Almighty God or does it prove the opposite? Are there several gods or is there only one? Why is there only one god? What is the logic to believe in only one god?

Then we move to the topic of creation. We try to understand the secret of life in a logical way. Why do we live? What is the purpose of this life? Why has Almighty God created us and put us in this world? What is the purpose of creating the whole universe? Both good and evil exist in our lives, but why has Almighty God created evil? Why not only good? Would our lives be better if evil had not been created?

A human being cannot be just a physical matter. Otherwise, we would be like stones, rocks or sand. There should be a spiritual part in us, which is responsible for thinking, feeling, imagining, memorising, etc. Thus, does the soul exist? What is the difference between the soul and the spirit? What is the proof of the existence of soul? Is the soul affected by time? Does the soul die when the physical body dies?

We further investigate the logic behind the need for the hereafter, paradise and hell. Is there proof of a next life after death? What is the logical proof for the hereafter? Do paradise and hell exist? Will non-Muslims go to paradise or hell?

Another important question is related to destiny and freedom of choice. If Almighty God knows everything and decides on everything, why would He judge our deeds? Do we choose our deeds or are they written for us? What are the things that we can choose and what are the things that we cannot choose?

The holy Quran is the last heavenly book revealed to prophet Mohammed Peace Be Upon Him (PBUH), after the Zabur revealed to Dawud PBUH, the Torah revealed to Moses PBUH and the Bible revealed to Jesus PBUH. Was the holy Quran written by the prophet Mohammed PBUH? Has prophet Mohammed PBUH copied the holy Quran from the Bible and the Torah? What is the miracle of the holy Quran? What is the logical proof that the holy Quran is from Almighty God?

The last topic in this book deals with the Islam. We provide logic answers to the following questions. Why Islam as religion? Why is Mohammed PBUH chosen to be prophet? Why is the prophet Mohammed PBUH the last messenger of Almighty God? Is the Tawaf (revolving around the house of Allah in Macca) a sort of worshipping stones?

In Arabic language, the name 'God' is 'Allah'. We will use the word 'God' and 'Allah' interchangeably in this book, i.e. there is no difference in meaning between 'God' and 'Allah'. However, the word 'god' starting with lower case does not necessarily mean 'Allah'. It is used in a general sense. We will add SWT (Subhanahu Wa Ta'ala, which means 'Glory to Him the Exalted') after the word 'Allah' and PBUH after the name of a prophet.

Quran verses are cited by chapter and verse numbers. For example, [37:96] means chapter 37, verse 96, and in case of multiple consecutive verses, [82:10-12] means chapter 82, verses 10 to 12.

The English translation of Quran verses presented in this book is mainly based on Shakir, Pickthal and Abdullah Yusufali from the following websites:

http://quran.al-islam.org/ and https://www.searchtruth.com/

The Hadith (sayings or records of traditions of the prophet Mohammed PBUH) translation is mainly from the website:

https://www.searchtruth.com/

Words of thanks

In the Name of Allah, Most Gracious, Most Merciful.

I would like to add some words of thanks and acknowledgements. Thanks to Allah SWT, Almighty God, the Lord of the Worlds '[1:2] *All praise is due to Allah, the Lord of the Worlds*'. Thanks to Allah SWT for everything He gives me in life '[16:18] *And if you would count Allah's favours, you will not be able to number them*'. Thanks to Allah SWT for giving me life and guiding me to the right path '[26:78] *Who created me, then He has shown me the way*'. Thanks to Allah SWT for asking us to seek knowledge and encouraging us to increase our knowledge '[20:114] *and say: O my Lord! Increase me in knowledge*'. Thanks to Allah SWT for sending messengers to us and for revealing to them holy books '[18:1] *(All) praise is due to Allah, Who revealed the Book to His servant and did not make in it any crookedness*'. Thanks to Allah SWT for showing us His signs so that we can recognise Him '[27:93] *And say: Praise be to Allah, He will show you His signs so that you shall recognize them*'.

I would like to thank Mr Mohammed Rafeat Abdel Motleb for initiating the first discussion over the idea of this book. His input and discussion on the different topics and questions presented in this book are highly acknowledged.

Special thanks go my daughter Mona Abdel Wahab for translating this book from English to Dutch. Her efforts and enthusiasm are highly appreciated.

Finally, I would like to thank the Muslim community in Ghent, Belgium, especially the brothers and sisters from mosque Badr, mosque Al-Mustaqbal and mosque Salah-El-Din, in which I have been acting as part-time Imam, delivering Friday speeches and leading Friday's prayers.

0 Introduction

Islam is a religion that invites believers and nonbelievers to think, understand, use logic and be rational to believe in Almighty God, recognise Him and remember Him. Islam is the last heavenly religion, which combines the spiritual belief with human intellect. It makes use of humans' intellect to support and strengthen their belief. The holy Quran is the last heavenly book, after the Torah and the Bible, revealed from Almighty God. It invites people to think about the creation of heavens and earth in order to recognise the creator and discover His greatness:

[3:190] *Most surely in the creation of the heavens and the earth and the alternation of the night and the day there are signs for men who understand.*

The term 'men who understand', refers to people who use their intellect, think logically and are rational. The word intellect or mind (in Arabic 'Akal') has been mentioned in the holy Quran 49 times, which indicates its importance. Thinking about the creation, and recognising how great it is, indicates and confirms the greatness of the creator. Furthermore, understanding the creation leads to belief in one god. After thinking and understanding, these people, who are mentioned in the above verse, remember Allah SWT and supplicate to Him.

[3:191] *Those who remember Allah standing and sitting and lying on their sides and reflect on the creation of the heavens and the earth: Our Lord! You have not created this in vain! Glory be to Thee; save us then from the chastisement of the fire.*

Thus, the holy Quran talks to people who think and use their mind, which is the general feature of all human beings of different levels. This indicates that the message of Islam is addressed to the intellect of all humans.

This universe is a great, perfect and complete system that indicates the infinite power of the creator. Allah SWT talks to people logically through the holy Quran and talks to their intellect:

[23:115-116] *What! Did you then think that We had created you in vain and that you shall not be returned to Us? So exalted be Allah, the True King; no god is there but He, the Lord of the Throne of Honour!*

Unlike other creatures, such as birds and animals, human beings were given the ability to think. Allah SWT chose humans for the test in this worldly life and gave them the freedom to choose between good and evil. Thus, only humans possess intellect, allowing them to recognise and worship Almighty God.

Worshipping Almighty God is not only done by praying and fasting, but also by remembering Him and thinking about His creations. Thinking is strongly related to seeking knowledge. Therefore, the holy Quran asks people to seek knowledge in all sciences and indicates that most people fearing Allah SWT are the scholars, who possess knowledge.

[35:28] *And of men and beasts and cattle are various species of it likewise; those of His servants only who are possessed of knowledge fear Allah; surely Allah is Mighty, Forgiving.*

The first verses revealed to the prophet PBUH were about knowledge, reading, learning and teaching.

[96:1-5] *Read in the name of your Lord Who created. He created man from a clot. Read and your Lord is Most Honourable. Who taught (to write) with the pen. Taught man what he knew not.*

The holy Quran encourages people to seek knowledge, not only in religion, but also in all different kinds of sciences. By asking people to look, consider and investigate the heavens and earth, it encourages them to explore the universe and research into astronomy and geology.

[7:185] *Do they not consider the kingdom of the heavens and the earth and whatever things Allah has created, and that may* be their doom shall have drawn nigh; what announcement would they then believe in after this?

The holy Quran also directs people to seek knowledge in human science, medicine and biology, by mentioning many verses describing the creation of human beings.

[86:5-7] *So let man consider of what he is created. He is created from a gushing fluid. Coming from between the backbone and the ribs.*

Similarly, thinking about plants, palms and trees, and how they grow from earth, open the door for research and investigation in the science of food and agriculture.

[80:24-32] *Then let man look to his food. That We pour down the water, pouring (it) down in abundance. Then, We cleave the earth, cleaving (it) asunder. Then, We cause to grow therein the grain. And grapes and clover. And the olive and the palm. And thick gardens. And fruits and herbage. A provision for you and for your cattle.*

The words 'look' and 'consider' in the above verses direct people to investigate and seek knowledge in these diverse topics of sciences. Knowledge is infinite and what we know so far, and what we will know in future is very limited indeed. When the prophet PBUH was asked by the Jews about the soul, the following Quran verse was revealed to indicate that the knowledge given to people is very little.

[17:85] *And they ask you about the soul. Say: The soul is one of the commands of my Lord, and you are not given aught of knowledge but a little.*

The human intellect is used to distinguish between good and evil, right and wrong, and to decide on different aspects of life and to choose directions. Every person has a different level of intellect. As Allah SWT is the most just, He will judge people according to their level of intellect.

The prophet PBUH mentioned that the actions of three kinds of people are not recorded, one of them a lunatic till he is restored to reason.

In Sunan Abudawd, the prophet PBUH said: There are three (people) whose actions are not recorded: a boy till he reaches puberty, a sleeper till he awakes, a lunatic till he is restored to reason. (Book #38, Hadith #4388)

This clearly means that only people possessing intellect are responsible for their deeds. People who do not have intellect will not be judged for their deeds. However, as mentioned above, all humans possess intellect, but with different levels ranging from very low to very high. Therefore, the holy Quran talks to people who have intellect.

[41:53] We will soon show them Our signs in the Universe and in their own souls, until it will become quite clear to them that it is the truth. Is it not sufficient as regards your Lord that He is a witness over all things?

The realisation of human being can be classified into two categories, namely, the visible world and the invisible world (the world of the unseen). The visible world is realised through the five physical common senses, which are hearing, sight, taste, touch and smell. However, the world of the unseen can only be realised through mind, intellect and messengers of Almighty God. Allah SWT is Knower of both worlds.

[59:22] He is Allah, than Whom there is no other Allah, the Knower of the Invisible and the Visible. He is the Beneficent, Merciful.

[72:26-27] The Knower of the unseen! so He does not reveal His secrets to any, Except to him whom He chooses as a messenger; for surely He makes a guard to march before him and after him.

The mind can be used to identify the unseen when its effect can be identified. For example, we use our mind to identify electricity, but we do not see it, as we just see its effect. Similarly, we do not see Almighty God, but we can identify His effects in the amazing creations of human being and universe. This is the reason why more than 1,300 verses in the holy Quran talk about the creation of man and universe. These verses clearly invite people to think and use their intellect to recognise Allah SWT.

When the effect of the unseen cannot be identified, the mind will not be able to work and the need of messengers from Almighty God becomes necessary. Therefore, Allah SWT has sent messengers throughout history to guide people to the right path.

The relationship between the mind and the revelation from Almighty God is essential and cannot be ignored. It is like the relationship between sight and light. Without light, the eyes are not able to see anything and a person becomes like a blind. Similarly, without revelation, the mind will not be able to recognise Allah SWT. Therefore, the mind is like sight and the revelation is like light. The mind has two tasks related to the revelation. The first one is to confirm that the revelation is from Allah SWT and the second one is to understand the revelation correctly without prejudicing it.

As Muslims, we believe that only Allah SWT has the knowledge of the world of the unseen and He reveals some of this knowledge through His messengers. However, this information of the unseen is not against the intellect and does not cancel it. Rather, it is above the intellect because the intellect of people is limited, but the unseen is unlimited and the knowledge of Almighty God is infinity.

There is a big difference between being against the intellect and being above the intellect. Being against the intellect will cancel the mind and stop people to think. However, being above the intellect opens the door for the mind to think and seek more knowledge. This is why the holy Quran is above the intellect of human being, but it is never against it.

The statement 'I see, I believe' means believing in the visible world and disbelieving in the world of the unseen. This statement, in fact, cancels the intellect of humans, therefore it is against the mind and is not a logical statement. We believe in lots of things around us, but we do not see them. We believe in oxygen in the air, but we do not see the oxygen. We believe in electricity, but we do not see electricity. We believe in radio waves and other waves, but we do not see them. Therefore, we believe in these unseen things by using our mind and logical thinking, and realising their effects.

The very far history and the future are both considered to be in the world of the unseen. If the concept of the statement 'I see, I believe' was said 150 years ago about the possibility to make an aircraft that flies between countries and continents or a rocket that goes to space, we would not have reached the technology that we have today. In fact, our intellect enables us to make logical conclusions about what will happen in the future in this world and in the hereafter.

There are two main categories of reasons that prevent human intellect to think about Almighty God and seek knowledge in religions. The first category is related to spiritual reasons, while the second category is related to external reasons. The spiritual reasons are divided into three main types, namely, desire, pride and insistence on sins.

Following desire means that people want to do what they like without any restriction or limitation. Therefore, they refuse to believe in Almighty God and religions, because believing will limit their desire.

[45:23] *Have you then considered him who takes his low desire for his god.*

Being arrogant is also preventing people from believing in Almighty God. Proud people do not want to submit to their Lord and admit His superiority. Allah SWT gives an example of the people of the prophet Noh PBUH in the holy Quran. They refused to listen to the messenger of Almighty God and closed their ears because of their arrogance.

[71:7] *And every time I have called to them, that Thou mightiest forgive them. They have (only) thrust their fingers into their ears, covered themselves up with their garments, grown obstinate, and given themselves up to arrogance.*

Insisting on sins is also a spiritual human characteristic related to being proud.

[2:6] *Surely those who disbelieve, it being alike to them whether you warn them, or do not warn them, will not believe.*

The external reason for not thinking about believing in Almighty God and following religions is related to the influence of society, environment and family. This is, in fact, the first obstacle that the prophet PBUH faced during delivering his message to his tribe. Children follow the religion of their parents without thinking and it becomes a part of their spiritual belief and common life. The holy Quran has encouraged people to overcome and resist this external obstacle by using their intellect.

[2:170] *And when it is said to them, Follow what Allah has revealed, they say: Nay! We follow what we found our fathers upon. What! And though their fathers had no sense at all, nor did they follow the right way.*

The strive between the intellect from one side and the spiritual and external reasons from the other side is the test from Almighty God in this worldly life. Every human has a certain level of intellect, has a specific soul and is influenced by certain society and family factors in his life. The test is then how he will use his intellect to overcome the spiritual and external obstacles, recognise and admit to the creator, Almighty God. As every person is different, every test is different and every model answer is different. Only Allah SWT can evaluate the results of the human tests, as He created these tests for us. As

Allah SWT is the most just, the test is within the ability of every human.

[2:286] *Allah does not impose upon any soul a duty but to the extent of its ability.*

In fact, a human consists of three components, namely 1) a mind that thinks, 2) a heart that feels and 3) a body that moves. Knowledge feeds the mind, love feeds the heart, and food and drink feed the body. If a human feeds all three components at the same time, he will have success in this worldly life and in the hereafter. The balance between the three components is the reason for success. But if a human feeds only one or two components, he will become extreme or abnormal. For example, a person who has a high level of intelligence, but no heart, will not be appreciated by most people. Similarly, a person who has a sweet heart but a very low level of intelligence will also not be appreciated by most people. However, the person who has a balance between a sweet heart and a high level of intelligence is the one who will be appreciated.

The holy Quran talks to both human mind and heart, like in the following verses, in which the first verse is directed to the heart, while the second to the mind.

[82:6] *O man! What hath made thee careless concerning thy Lord, the Bountiful.*

[82:7] *Who created thee, then fashioned, then proportioned thee?*

Therefore, Islam is a religion that combines heart and mind. Only mind or only heart is not enough to be fully convinced about Islam and about believing in Almighty God. Human beings need to understand with the mind and feel with the heart.

In this book, we make use of flowcharts to illustrate the logic in the different beliefs and Islamic concepts. We will mainly use the basic symbols of flowcharts, such as start, end, process and decision blocks, as illustrated in logic flowchart 0. The oval mirror blocks represent the start or the end of the logic flowchart. The rectangular block represents a process, task or operation. The diamond block is used for decision making with two options: yes or no.

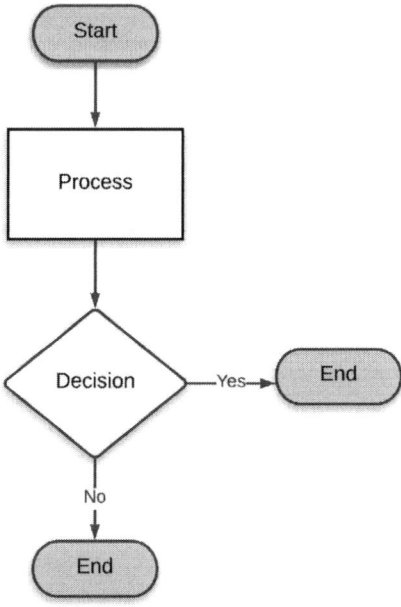

Logic flowchart 0: Basic symbols of flowcharts used in this book

We will further make use of the Laws of Logic, also known as the Laws of Thoughts, originally introduced by Aristotle.[1] We will mainly use the first two principles of the Law of Thoughts, namely the Law of Identity and the Law of Non-Contradiction.

The Law of Identity: It states that, if a statement has been determined to be true, then the statement is true. This means that a statement telling a fact is a true statement and any other statement telling the opposite to this fact violates the Law of

---

1 Ancient Greek philosopher, 384-322BC.

Identity and is not a logical statement. For example, a statement saying 'the earth is revolving around the sun' is a fact. Thus, a statement saying 'the earth is not revolving around the sun' is against the Law of Identity and leads to a non-logical conclusion.

The Law of Non-Contradiction: It states that nothing can both be and not be. This means that two statements contradicting one another cannot be both true at the same time. If an idea is described by two contradictory statements, it violates the Law of Non-Contradiction and is not logical. For example, a statement saying that 'nature creates new nature' contradicts the statement saying that 'new nature will not create another new nature'. Therefore, the argument that 'nature creates nature' is against the Law of Non-Contradiction and leads to a non-logical conclusion.

1   Almighty God (Allah SWT)

1.1   What is the logic in the existence of Almighty God?

To demonstrate the logic in the existence of Almighty God, we consider some examples from our lives. For example, if someone finds a glass cup on the street, would it be possible that he thinks that the cup just existed by itself or made itself? Logically, he will think that it has been made by someone. In fact, it will have gone through a manufacturing process, from design right through until the production of its final shape. Similarly, if you see a building, it is impossible to think that it was found like that or it was built by itself. There would have been an engineer, who designed the building and contractors, who implemented the design of the engineer.

Similar to the two examples of glass cup and building described above, everything around us has an origin and was made by some power. Chairs, tables, cars and airplanes have been designed and manufactured somewhere and by someone. We can even identify the manufacturer of products by looking at them. For example, if we look at a car, we can recognise its manufacturer, e.g. Mercedes, BMW or Opel.

Similarly, if we look at Earth, Sun, Moon, Stars and Galaxies, is it possible to think that they are there without a designer and a manufacturer (creator)? Where do they come from? How do they move relative to each other? How were they designed? Based on logic that any product has been made by someone, we have to accept that Earth and Heaven were created by a super power, Almighty God.

In logic flowchart 1, a comparison is made between the construction of a building and the creation of the universe. The statement saying that a building needs to be built by a builder or an engineer is a fact. Similarly, the statement saying that the universe must have been created by a creator is also a fact. Therefore, the opposite statement saying that a building can be constructed by itself or the universe can have been created by itself is against the Law of Identity.

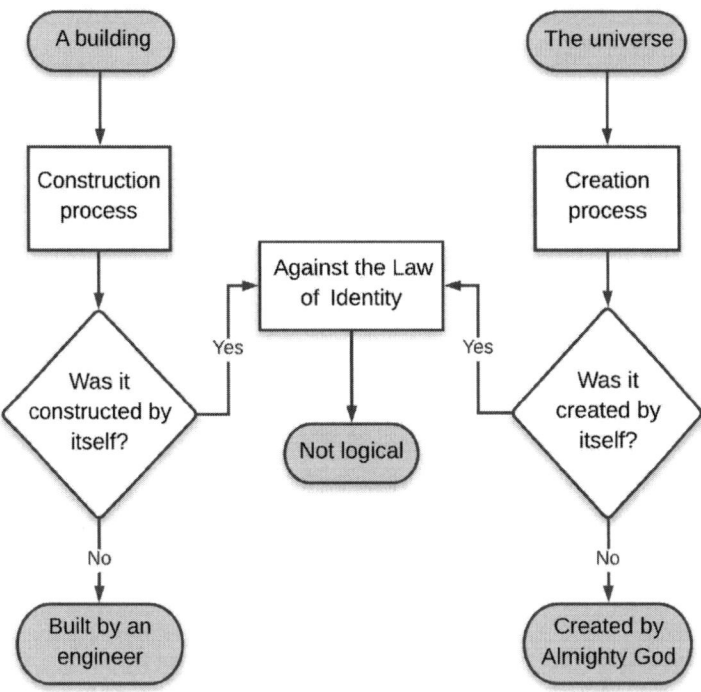

Logic flowchart 1: Existence of Almighty God – Example 1

Allah SWT talks about this concept logically in the holy Quran and asks people who created them, and who created the earth and the heavens? Have they been created by themselves?

[52:35-36] *Were they created of nothing, or were they themselves the creators? Or did they create the heavens and the earth? Nay, they have no firm belief.*

Consider another example: if we imagine that the universe is like a machine and we open this machine, we will see that the elements are linked by gears and mechanical parts. Can anyone say that these gears and mechanical parts were made by themselves? They have obviously been designed and made by an engineer to hold the machine's elements together.

Likewise, if we look at the universe, we see that galaxies, planets and stars are linked to each other by gravity and relativity. It is then logical to conclude that gravity and relativity have not been made by themselves, but that they have been created by a superpower, Almighty God, to hold the parts of the universe, i.e. stars and galaxies, together.

In logic flowchart 2, a comparison is made between machine elements on the one side and galaxies and stars on the other side. The machine elements are linked to each other through gears and mechanical parts, and the galaxies and stars are linked to each other through gravity and relativity. The statement saying that gears and mechanical parts should be made by an engineer is a fact. Similarly, the statement saying that gravity and relativity should have been made by a creator is a fact. Therefore, the opposite statement saying that gears and mechanical parts can be made by themselves or saying that galaxies and stars could have been made by themselves is against the Law of Identity.

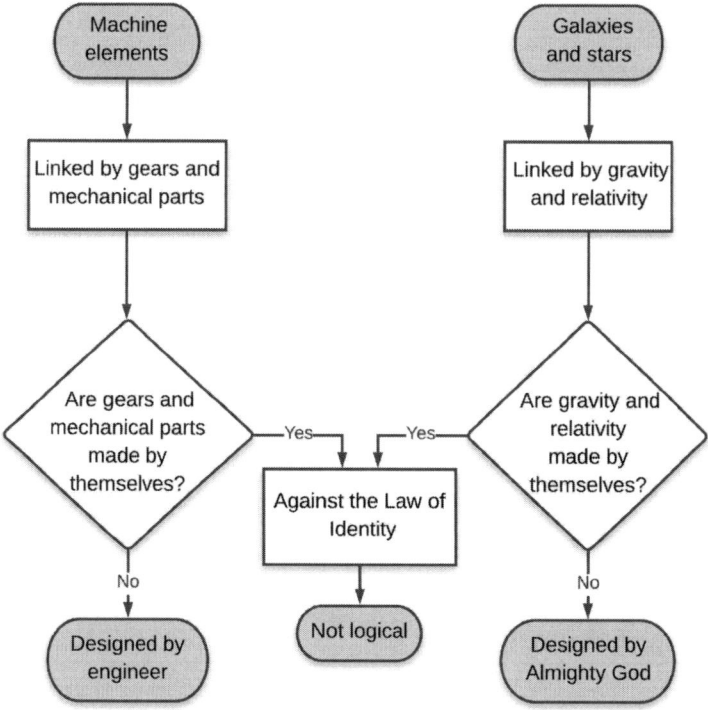

Logic flowchart 2: Existence of Almighty God – Example 2

We can recognise Almighty God using our mind, but we cannot see him with our eyes. This is because recognising Almighty God and worshipping Him is a test for all mankind. If people could see Almighty God with their eyes, there would be no test and all humans would be believers. For example, if a student sitting an examination received the model answers to the questions during the examination, would this be a fair examination? The wisdom of the examiner implies that the student should only receive the exam questions and not the answers. Similarly, the wisdom of Allah SWT implies that we should not see Him so that we receive only the questions of our test and we should look for the answers by ourselves.

A comparison between a student's exam and a human's test is shown in logic flowchart 3. At the beginning of the exam, a student receives the questions related to his course subject. Similarly, a human undergoes a test during his life to recognise his creator. The statement saying that the student should not get the answers to the exam questions at the beginning of or during the examination is a fact. Likewise, the statement saying that a human should not see his creator during this worldly life, i.e. should not get the answer to the test of his life, is a fact. Therefore, the opposite statement saying that the student should get the answers during the exam or saying that a human should see his creator during his life is against the Law of Identity.

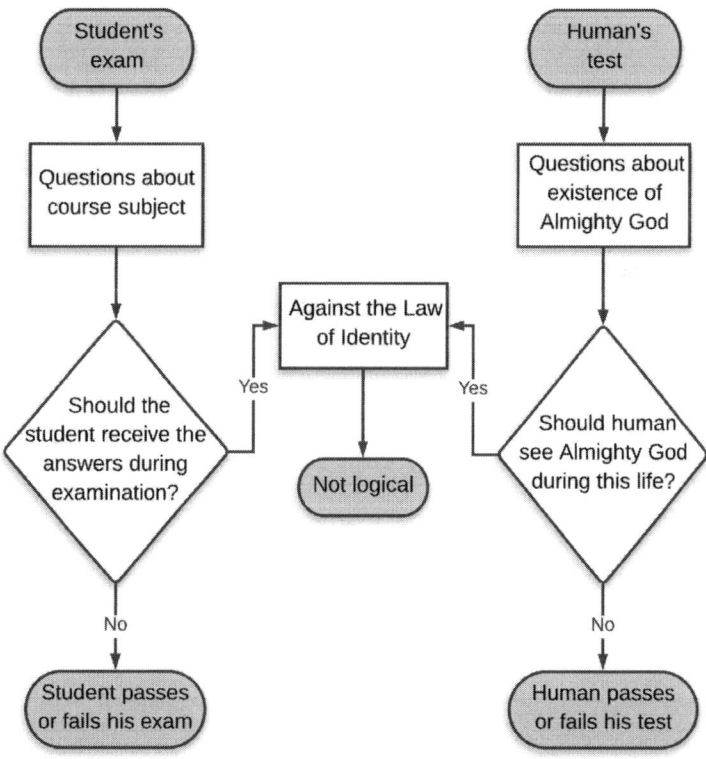

Logic flowchart 3: Existence of Almighty God – Example 3

A further important note is that the physical body of humans does not have the capability to see Almighty God. Allah SWT is the most seeing and the most hearing, as He created our eyes and ears with limited capacity. His seeing and hearing capacity is therefore infinite and cannot be compared to those of humans or any other creatures. Therefore, He can see us, but we cannot see Him.

[6:103] *No vision can grasp Him, but His grasp is over all vision: He is above all comprehension, yet is acquainted with all things.*

Even prophets and messengers could not see Almighty God and their messages were always revealed through angel Gabriel. They could not even talk to Almighty God except through revelation or behind a screen because He is very high and the difference between Him and His creatures is like the distance between the heavens and the earth. Therefore, a human cannot withstand the power of Allah SWT if he sees Him or talks directly with Him, as he would fall into a swoon due to the extremely strong power of Almighty God.

[42:51] *And it is not for any mortal that Allah should speak to him except by revelation or from behind a veil, or by sending a messenger and revealing by His permission what He pleases; surely He is High, Wise.*

As an example, we cannot touch a high-voltage electricity cable directly with our hand because of its high power. One would immediately die if one did. But if we use an isolation layer around the cable, we can touch it. Similarly, if one gets closer to the sun, one will be burned and become blind. The distance and space between us and the sun are acting as screens to protect us from its high power.

The prophet Musa PBUH talked with Almighty God (from behind a screen), but he did not see Him. Musa PBUH asked to see Almighty God, but His answer was that he could not bear to see Him. To prove this fact to Musa PBUH, Allah SWT manifested to the mountain, which was not able to bear the power of Allah SWT and was destroyed.

[7:143] *And when Musa came at Our appointed time and his Lord spoke to him, he said: My Lord! show me (Thyself), so that I may look upon Thee. He said: You cannot (bear to) see Me but look at the mountain, if it remains firm in its place, then will you see Me; but when his Lord manifested His glory to the mountain He made it crumble and Musa fell down in a swoon; then when he recovered, he said: Glory be to Thee, I turn to Thee, and I am the first of the believers.*

I asked a nine-year old girl about Almighty God. She said my parents are atheists, so I do not believe in any god. I then asked her "And who created you?" She answered, "My mother, because I come from the tummy of my mother." I asked again "And who created your mother?" She answered, "My grandmother." I said, "So, if we go back in time, we will find that every mother was created by her mother, until we reach the first woman on earth. Who created this first woman?" She had to think for a while and then said, "Nature!" I said, "But who created nature?"

Can nature create nature? Is nature god? This is the next question in this chapter.

1.2 Is nature god?

A logical argument that proves that nature is not god and nature cannot create nature is as follows. We start with the assumption that the cause of nature can be either natural or non-natural (supernatural). However, the cause of nature cannot be natural because this would be circular fallacy (logical fallacy or circular logic, i.e. ending up at the beginning). A fallacy means the use of invalid reasoning to construct a concept. Therefore, the cause of nature has to be non-natural (supernatural), i.e. Almighty God.

This concept is illustrated in logic flowchart 4. If we assume that nature creates new nature, we can ask if new nature can create another new nature, and if this new nature can create another new nature. In other words, this action can be repeated up to infinity with no beginning and no end. The statement saying that nature has a beginning and an end is a scientific fact. Therefore, the statement saying that nature has no beginning and no end is against the Law of Identity. Furthermore, if nature can create new nature, the statement saying that new nature cannot create another new nature is against the Law of Non-Contradiction.

Nature depends on time as it keeps changing throughout history. Time, by definition, should have a beginning and an end. We further assume that the cause of time can be either dependent on time or not. Again, the cause of time cannot be dependent on time because this would be a circular fallacy. Therefore, the cause of time should be independent of time.

As Allah SWT created the cause of time, i.e. the earth, sun and moon, He created time and He should be independent of time. Furthermore, it is logically impossible for an object independent of time to be caused by something, i.e. there is no temporal beginning in front of which to put a cause. Therefore, the logical conclusion is that the cause of nature, Allah SWT, is supernatural, timeless and uncaused.

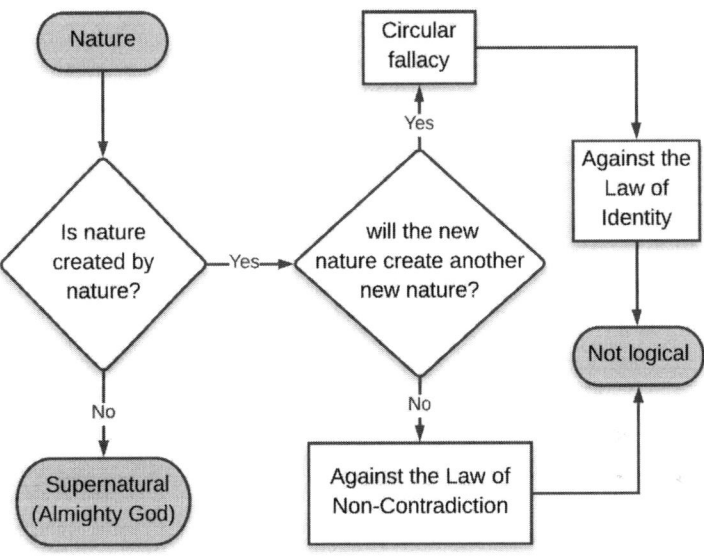

Logic flowchart 4: Nature – Example 1

The concept of the cause of time is illustrated in logic flowchart 5. If we assume that time is dependent on a second time, we can ask if the second time would be dependent on a third time. If the second time is dependent on the third time, this action can be repeated up to infinity with no beginning and no end. As the statement saying that time has a beginning and an end is a fact, the statement saying that time has no beginning and no end is against the Law of Identity. Furthermore, if time is dependent on a second time, the statement saying that the second time is not dependent on the third time is against the Law of Non-Contradiction.

Nature is a fact and not an explanation, as what we discover in nature does not explain how it happens. As scientists said, nature does not explain, but is itself in need for explanation. For example, we know that rain falls because of evaporation of seawater, but we cannot explain how this is made to happen. In other words,

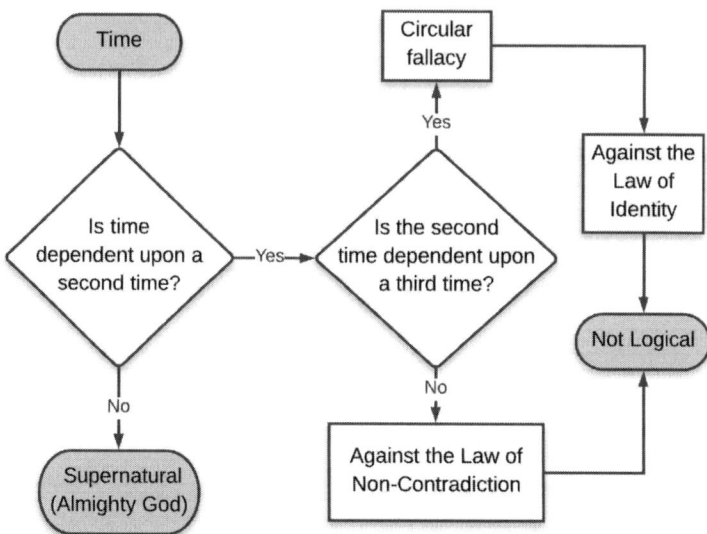

Logic flowchart 5: Nature – Example 2

what makes the water evaporate? It is the law of nature, but who made or created the law of nature?

The proof of existence of Almighty God can be seen in nature itself, e.g. in the cosmos system, in the human body, in a tree or a palm, in a butterfly or a bird, in a plant or a flower, and in the perfection and accuracy of creatures and creation. Saying that all of these came to exist by chance, is the same as throwing numbers in the air and thinking that they will be arranged in ascending or descending order without someone doing so.

A further argument about nature creating nature is as follows. If we assume that nature can create nature, we have to believe that nature is god. But god should be physical and spiritual at the same time. A creator cannot be only physical, i.e. nature, as he should be above the physical world, control it, manage it and not be part of it.

This concept is illustrated in logic flowchart 6. If we assume that nature creates nature, we can ask if a creator can be only physical, but not spiritual. As a human has physical and spiritual elements, the statement saying that the creator should be physical and spiritual is a fact. Therefore, the statement saying that the creator should only be physical, i.e. nature, is against the Law of Identity.

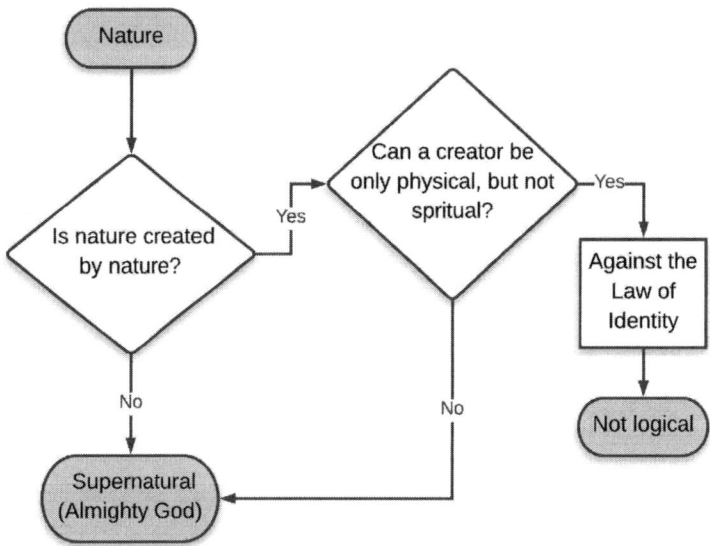

Logic flowchart 6: Nature – Example 3

The holy Quran talks about the nature and clearly describes its origin and its purpose. Allah SWT has created nature and made it subservient to humans. He made everything in nature available for us to use. Indeed, we use rivers and seas for travel and obtain beneficial substances and matters from them. We use the heat of the sun and the light of the moon in our daily lives and we use the stars to direct us to the right way. Therefore, everything in nature is indeed for us and for our benefit.

[16:14-17] *And He it is Who has made the sea subservient that you may eat fresh flesh from it and bring forth from it ornaments which you wear, and you see the ships cleaving through it, and that you might seek of His bounty and that you may give thanks.*

And He has cast great mountains in the earth lest it might be convulsed with you, and rivers and roads that you may go aright. And landmarks; and by the stars they find the right way. Is He then Who creates like him who does not create? Do you not then mind?

In fact, nature itself is proof of the existence of Almighty God. When the nonbelievers of the tribe of the prophet Mohammed PBUH (Quraysh) asked him about a miracle from Almighty God, so that they would believe in his message, Allah SWT has revealed the following verses.

[2:164] *Most surely in the creation of the heavens and the earth and the alternation of the night and the day, and the ships that run in the sea with that which profits men, and the water that Allah sends down from the cloud, then gives life with it to the earth after its death and spreads in it all (kinds of) animals, and the changing of the winds and the clouds made subservient between the heaven and the earth, there are signs for a people who understand. This indicates that the greatest miracle, which stays forever, is the nature and the world around us as there are infinite number of proves and signs showing the existence and greatness of Almighty God.*

The holy Quran refers to the corruption of nature, i.e. pollution and climate change, which are two of the biggest challenges to humans nowadays. It indicates that climate change is a consequence of the bad deeds of mankind on earth.

[30:41] *Corruption doth appear on land and sea because of (the evil) which men's hands have done, that He may make them taste a part of that which they have done, in order that they may return.*

In the above verse, the land and the sea can be understood as referring to nature. Therefore, the corruption in nature refers to pollution, climate change and everything abnormal in nature. The verse also indicates that this corruption in nature is done by humans, i.e. the hands of mankind. Indeed, scientists of today have confirmed that people are responsible for pollution and climate change. The verse further warns people and asks them to stop what they are doing to nature, and to focus on and work to repair the damage they have caused. This is similar to the warning of United Nation and worldwide climate change organisations. It is amazing to see that this warning in the holy Quran, which was revealed more than 1400 years ago.

As nature cannot create nature, can life be created by nature? Who has designed life on earth? How are the different measures perfectly chosen to allow us to live on this earth? Can life come to existence without a designer? Can life be designed by chance? Or is it designed by Almighty God? We answer these questions in the next section.

1.3 Can life be designed by chance or without a designer?

The life on the earth is made possible by many measures. For example, the distance between the earth and the sun is perfect to permit life. Major changes in the distance between them would affect the average temperature on earth and life would not be possible.

Furthermore, if the distance between the sun and the earth was increased threefold, the force of gravity, i.e. the attraction of the sun would be one ninth of what it is today. As Jupiter is much closer to the earth, it would pull the earth with a force stronger than that of the sun. Thus, the earth would be irreversibly ejected from the solar system.

Likewise, the distance between the earth and the moon is perfect for humans to live on earth. If the distance between the earth and the moon was decreased by half, tides would be much higher and tidal forces from the moon would be eight times stronger. If the moon was, for example, 20 times closer, it would exert a gravitational force 400 times greater than what we are used to, and a huge tidal bulge would be created, hitting the land and causing great flooding, which would make life on earth impossible.

These relative distances between the earth, the sun and the moon are perfectly designed for life and therefore, there has to be a designer with an infinite intelligence, beyond human imagination, and superior power above all His creatures.

This concept is further illustrated in logic flowchart 7. The statement saying that the distances between sun and earth, and moon and earth, are perfect for life is a fact. Therefore, the statement saying that they are not is against the Law of Identity and is not logical.

humans, i.e. the hands of mankind. Indeed, scientists of today have confirmed that people are responsible for pollution and climate change. The verse further warns people and asks them to stop what they are doing to nature, and to focus on and work to repair the damage they have caused. This is similar to the warning of United Nation and worldwide climate change organisations. It is amazing to see that this warning in the holy Quran, which was revealed more than 1400 years ago.

As nature cannot create nature, can life be created by nature? Who has designed life on earth? How are the different measures perfectly chosen to allow us to live on this earth? Can life come to existence without a designer? Can life be designed by chance? Or is it designed by Almighty God? We answer these questions in the next section.

1.3 Can life be designed by chance or without a designer?

The life on the earth is made possible by many measures. For example, the distance between the earth and the sun is perfect to permit life. Major changes in the distance between them would affect the average temperature on earth and life would not be possible.

Furthermore, if the distance between the sun and the earth was increased threefold, the force of gravity, i.e. the attraction of the sun would be one ninth of what it is today. As Jupiter is much closer to the earth, it would pull the earth with a force stronger than that of the sun. Thus, the earth would be irreversibly ejected from the solar system.

Likewise, the distance between the earth and the moon is perfect for humans to live on earth. If the distance between the earth and the moon was decreased by half, tides would be much higher and tidal forces from the moon would be eight times stronger. If the moon was, for example, 20 times closer, it would exert a gravitational force 400 times greater than what we are used to, and a huge tidal bulge would be created, hitting the land and causing great flooding, which would make life on earth impossible.

These relative distances between the earth, the sun and the moon are perfectly designed for life and therefore, there has to be a designer with an infinite intelligence, beyond human imagination, and superior power above all His creatures.

This concept is further illustrated in logic flowchart 7. The statement saying that the distances between sun and earth, and moon and earth, are perfect for life is a fact. Therefore, the statement saying that they are not is against the Law of Identity and is not logical.

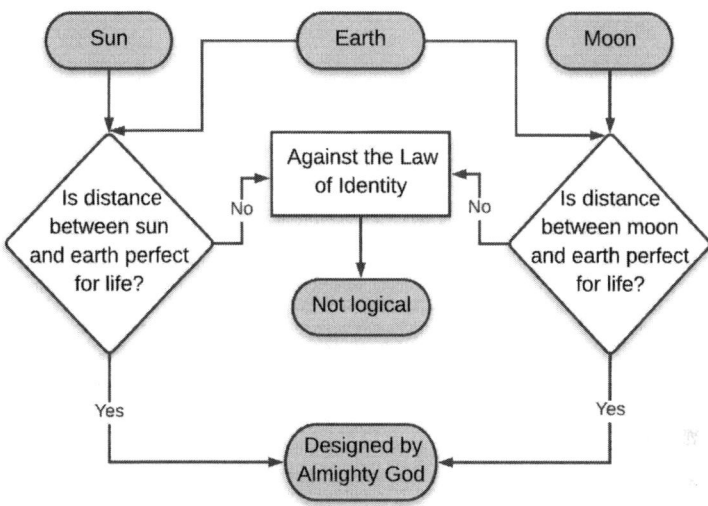

Logic flowchart 7: Design of life – Example 1

Furthermore, the size of the earth is perfectly designed. If the earth was smaller or larger than it is now, it would be impossible to live on it. For example, if the size of the earth was equal to the size of the moon, i.e. its diameter was one fourth its real diameter, its gravity would be one sixth its real gravity, in which case, air and water would not stay on the earth and would disappear. It would be very cold during the night, very hot during the day, and life would be impossible.

On contrast, if the size of the earth was twice its real size, i.e. its diameter was two times its real diameter, the atmospheric pressure on earth would be two times higher. Its mass would increase eight times, its gravity would be twice as strong and life would be very difficult. If the earth was as large as the sun, the atmospheric pressure would increase tremendously and life on earth would be impossible.

Another proof of the earth's perfect design can be seen in the perfect composition of air and the quantity of oxygen it contains. Air consists of 20.95% oxygen. If this percentage was higher, fires would spread faster. Fire in one tree would be enough to burn an entire forest. Giant insects would be alive and we would die younger because of oxidative stress. In contrast, if the percentage of oxygen was lower, we would suffer from poor muscular coordination, rapid fatigue and irregular respiration.

Amazingly, the holy Quran mentions the relationship between oxygen and fires. In the following verse, Allah SWT mentions that He made for us the green plants and trees to help ignite fire.

[36:80] *He Who has made for you the fire (to burn) from the green tree, so that with it you kindle (fire).*

As combustion requires both oxygen and fuel, the green tree is clearly referring to the production of oxygen. Usually, wood from hard or dry trees is used for the ignition of fire, so the use of green trees indicates the need of oxygen for combustion. Thus, the amount of oxygen in air is just enough for us to use fire in a safe way for our benefit.

Water is another substance designed perfectly for life. It is in fact the secret of life; without water there would be no life on earth. Everything alive is created from water. This is not only a scientific fact, but it is also mentioned in the holy Quran.

[21:30] *We have made of water everything living, will they not then believe?*

[24:45] *And Allah has created from water every living creature: so of them is that which walks upon its belly, and of them is that which walks upon two feet, and of them is that which walks upon four; Allah creates what He pleases; surely Allah has power over all things.*

The density of water is perfectly designed as it is in its solid state, less than in its liquid state. In other words, ice is less dense than water. Therefore, water is a unique liquid because, contrary to other liquids, it becomes less dense when it freezes. As a result, ice floats to the top instead of sinking to the bottom. This phenomenon makes water very valuable for life on Earth. As ice forms on the surface of rivers and seas, it protects the water underneath from consolidation and keeps the water temperature below freezing so that water creatures could survive.

Logic flowchart 8 shows the concept of the perfect quantity of oxygen in air and the perfect density of water. The statement saying that the percentage of oxygen in air is the correct percentage required for life is a fact. Likewise, the statement saying that the density of water is perfectly suitable for life is also a fact. Therefore, the statement saying that the percentage of oxygen in air is not the correct percentage required for life is against the Law of Identity. Similarly, the statement that the density of water is not perfectly suitable for life is also against the Law of Identity.

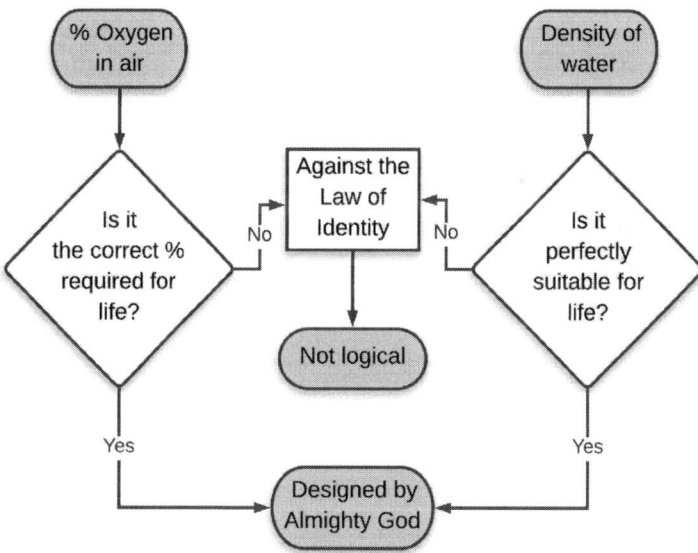

Logic flowchart 8: Design of life – Example 2

A computer program is made up of ones and zeros, i.e. 110010101011000. It is a binary code that uses the binary digits 0 and 1 to represent numbers, digits or any other characters defined in an electronic device. This binary code, which also provides the device with processor instructions, is programmed by an IT engineer and it is not possible to assume that it was found by chance or by itself.

Similarly, the information of DNA is stored as a specific code, which is made up of four chemical bases, namely A (adenine), T (thymine), G (guanine) and C (cytosine). These are arranged in the human cell as: CGTGTGACTCGCTCCTGAT, and so on. A genome, which is an organism containing genetic instructions, consists of 3.2 billion bases of DNA. These 3.2 billion DNA bases are repeated in specific sequences. Every person has a unique genome, i.e. unique DNA sequences, except for twins. Who or what could place this enormous number of letter combinations in their correct sequence for each person? Who or what could arrange the sequences of DNA in every different genome for each organism including bacteria, plant or animal?

In logic flowchart 9, a comparison is made between the binary code programmed in a computer and DNA code programmed in the human body. The statement saying that a binary code needs to be programmed by a programmer or an IT engineer is a fact. Similarly, the statement saying that DNA code for each human needs to be programmed by the creator of the human body is also a fact. Therefore, the opposite statement saying that a binary code or a program can be programmed by itself or saying that the DNA code can be programmed by itself is against the Law of Identity.

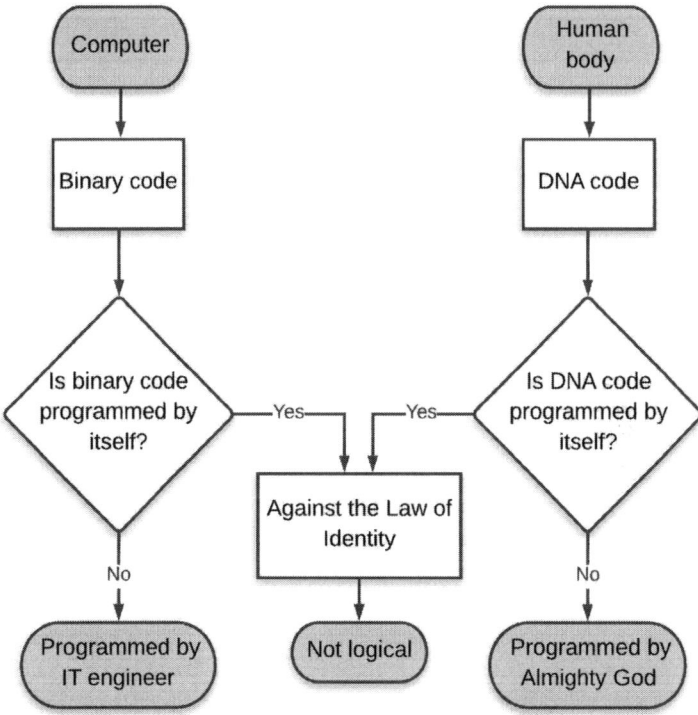

Logic flowchart 9: Design of life – Example 3

It is scientifically impossible to assume that the human genome has come to existence by chance. This is what mathematics tells us. If we want to arrange the numbers from 1 to 10 in ascending order – 1, 2, 3, …, 10 – the probability is calculated as $1/10! = 1/(1\times2\times3\times \times10) = 1/(3,628,800)$. This means that we would have to try more than 3 million times in order to arrange the numbers from 1 to 10. The chance that we would be able to succeed is $1/(3,628,800) = 2.756\times10^{-7}$.

As there are 3.2 billion DNA bases in a genome and they are repeated in specific sequences for each individual, the probability that they are arranged in the correct order is approximately $1/(3\times10)^9! = 1/1\times2\times3\times .\times(3\times10)^9 \approx 10^{-27}$. This means that, to arrange these nucleotides in the correct order, an astronomical number of trials is required and the chance to order them correctly is quasi-zero. Therefore, you, I and the other 7.5 billion people currently living on this earth cannot come to existence by chance. Every one of us is made to be that specific person with all his details.

As shown in logic flowchart 10, the 3.2 billion DNA bases are arranged in a specific way for each individual person. The statement saying that the probability that they were arranged correctly by chance is quasi-zero, is a fact, as explained above. Therefore, the statement saying that the probability is not quasi-zero, is against the Law of Identity.

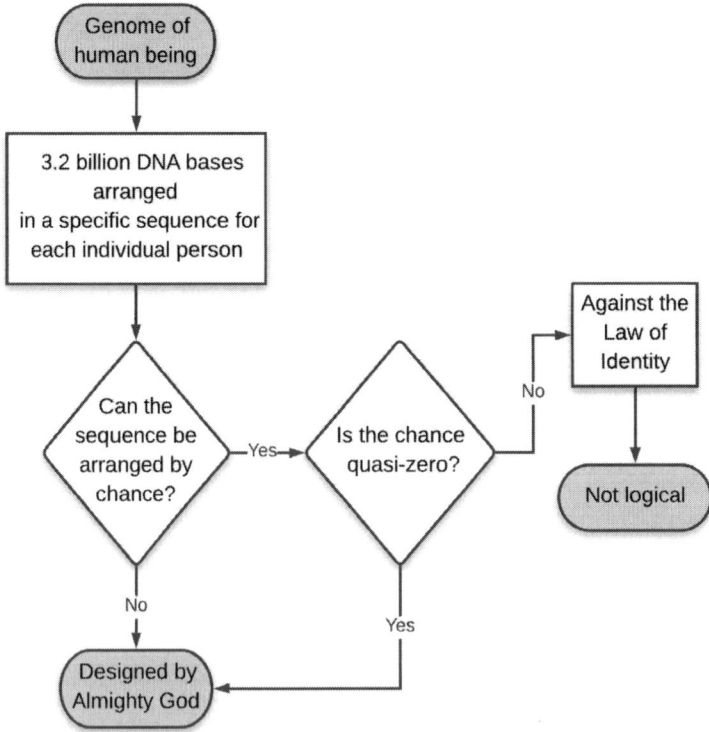

Logic flowchart 10: Design of life – Example 4

As life cannot be designed and created without Almighty God, how does Almighty God come to existence? If everything is created, how is Almighty God created? Who created Almighty God? This is the next question in this chapter.

1.4 Who created Almighty God?

The question itself is not logical. A creator, Almighty God, per definition, cannot be created, and if we assume that He is, a circular fallacy will be produced. As Almighty God is not created, we cannot ask who created Almighty God and the question becomes self-contradictory.

It is not coherent to argue that the universe was created by one god, but this one god was in turn created by god to the second power, who was in turn created by god to the third power, thus creating a chain to infinity with no end. As argued by scientists, there must be a reality that causes, but is itself uncaused (or a being that moves but is itself unmoved) because, if there is an infinite regression of causes, by definition, the whole process could never begin.

Another reason why this question is not logical is that Allah SWT does not follow the laws of his creatures. Rather, He has made these laws for us to live in time and space, but He is above time and space. Thus, it is not logical to apply the laws of life to Him, because He created them.

In logic flowchart 11, we assume that god is created by another god, and then we ask if another god will be created by another higher-order god. If the higher-order god creates another god, this action can be repeated up to infinity with no beginning and no end. In such a case, god is defined as creator and creature at the same time. As the statement saying that a creature has a beginning and an end is a fact, the statement saying that a creature has no beginning and no end (infinitely repeated, i.e. circular fallacy) is against the Law of Identity. Furthermore, as the original statement saying that god is created by another god, the statement saying that another god is not created by another higher-order god is against the Law of Non-Contradiction.

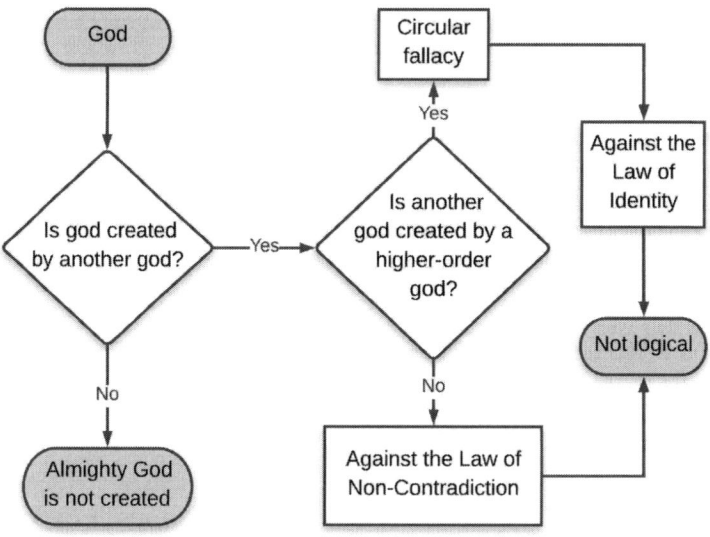

Logic flowchart 11: Who created Almighty God – Example 1

The logic implies that all creatures are created by one creator who is not created. Every creation has a beginning and an end. However, Almighty God is in a different category, different from all nature, humanity and everything that exists, in that He has always existed, independent from anything He created. He is the first before all His creatures, He is the last after all His creatures, He is the highest above all His creatures and He is the Knower of everything about His creatures in heavens and on earth.

[57:3] *He is the First and the Last and the Ascendant (over all) and the Knower of hidden things, and He is Cognizant of all things.*

The prophet Mohammed PBUH also used to say in his prayer "Allah You are the first and nothing was before You, and You are the last and nothing will be after You". He has also mentioned in one Hadith that before the creation, there was only Allah SWT.

Narrated Imran bin Hussain: The prophet PBUH said, "There was Allah SWT and nothing else before Him and His Throne was over the water, and He then created the Heavens and the Earth and wrote everything in the Book." (Book #93, Hadith #514)

The argument 'How Almighty God created Himself' is also an illogical question that is self-contradictory because it assumes that Almighty God can be created. However, as we mentioned before, a creator, per definition, cannot be created. The existence of Almighty God does not have a beginning and does not have an end, but it is rather a self-characteristic of Allah SWT. His existence is forever and is above time and space, as He has created both time and space. Allah SWT is not a dependent being. Instead, as described in the holy Quran, Allah SWT is self-sufficient and self-existent.

[112:1-4] Say: He, Allah, is One. Allah is He on Whom all depend. He begets not, nor is He begotten. And none is like Him.

In logic flowchart 12, we assume that god is begotten, and then we ask if the father of god will be begotten as well. If the father of god is begotten, this action can be repeated up to infinity with no beginning and no end. In such a case, god is defined as father and son at the same time. As the statement saying that a father or son has a beginning and an end is a fact, the statement saying that a father or son has no beginning and no end (infinitely repeated, i.e. circular fallacy) is against the Law of Identity. Furthermore, as the original statement saying that god is begotten, the statement saying that the father of god is not begotten is against the Law of Non-Contradiction.

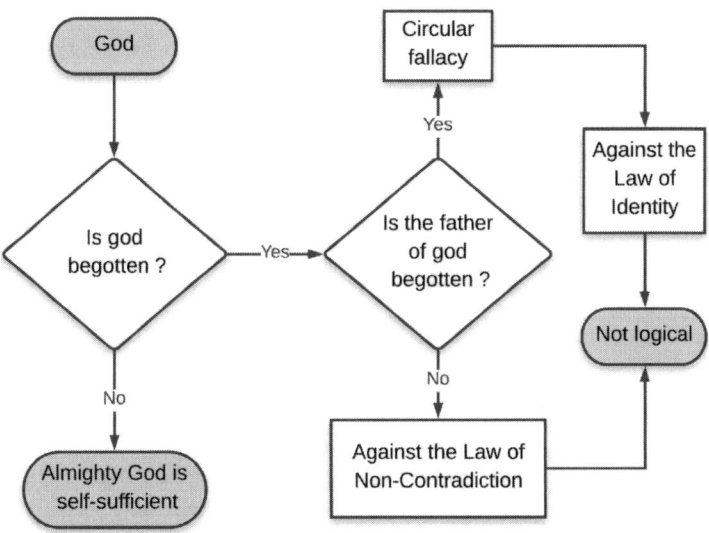

Logic flowchart 12: Who created Almighty God – Example 2

As Almighty God begets not, nor is He begotten, He has no father, son or a partner, why should there be only one god? What is the logic of the existence of only one god? Why is there not more than one god? What is the proof of the existence of only one god? The answers to these questions will be provided in the next section.

1.5 Why only one god?

All living things on earth, i.e. humans and animals, survive on water. Their bodies contain a large amount of water and they need water to survive. They also share common needs, such as food, sleep, air and oxygen. They all need food to live and grow, they get rid of their waste and they need solar energy. This similarity indicates that there should be one creator. As mentioned earlier in this chapter, the holy Quran, which was revealed more than

1,400 years ago, states that Allah SWT created every living thing from water.

This concept is illustrated in logic flowchart 13. The statement saying that all living things are made of water and need water to survive is a fact. This indicates that the creator of all living thing should be the same, i.e. only one god. The opposite statement saying that they are not made of water or they do not need water to survive, is against the Law of Identity.

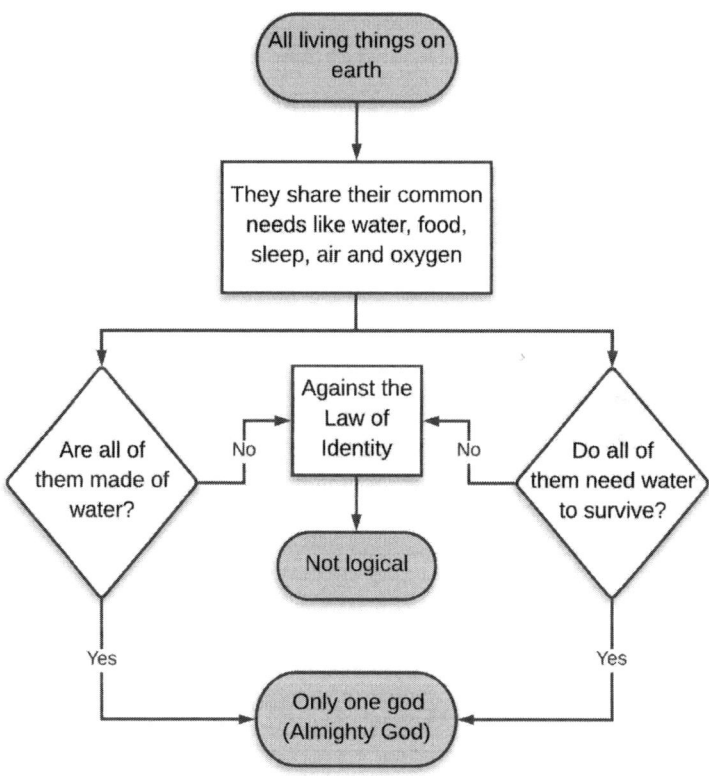

Logic flowchart 13: Only one god – Example 1

Due to advances in science and technology, it is now well known that all living things, including humans, animals, plants and organisms, are made up of cells. A cell contains most of the water in a human body. The estimated percentage of water in an adult human body is 60%. All cells in all living things have the same structures, which consist of a nucleus and a cell wall. Furthermore, all living things store genetic information using the same molecules, which are DNA and ribonucleic acid (RNA). This further confirms the similarity in their creation.

Furthermore, all organisms and all living things have life cycles, including birth, grow reproduction and death. They all have a start (beginning), a process during life and an end. This similarity also indicates the uniqueness of the creator and confirms that there can only be one creator, Almighty God.

[30:54] *Allah is He Who created you from a state of weakness then He gave strength after weakness, then ordained weakness and hoary hair after strength; He creates what He pleases, and He is the Knowing, the Powerful.*

Furthermore, the dependence of the different living things on each other and their need for each other for their survival demonstrates the perfect design of life by one god. The plants grow from seeds and make their food from the soil and ground. The animals eat plants, and in some cases other animals to survive. The food of humans depends on plants as well as animals. After death, humans' and animals' bodies become dust and return to the ground. This cycle and dependence of living things on each other proves that the creator is one.

We can also see the amazing similarity between creatures and systems in our world and in the universe. At atom level, electrons revolve around the nucleus. At astronomical level, in the solar system, planets revolve around the sun, and the stars revolve around the centre of the galaxy. Does this not demonstrate that the creator is one?

If there was more than one god, they would disagree, fight and destroy the whole universe. We would also see a major contradiction in the creation. If one god wanted something and the other god wanted something else, what would happen? Which one of the two would enforce his opinion? If they started to fight, we would see a major war in the heavens. Allah SWT makes this clear in the holy Quran.

[23:91] *Never did Allah take to Himself a son, and never was there with him any (other) god, in that case would each god have certainly taken away what he created, and some of them would certainly have overpowered others; glory be to Allah above what they describe!*

[21:22] *If there had been in them (in earth and heavens) any gods except Allah, they would both have certainly been in a state of disorder; therefore glory be to Allah, the Lord of the dominion, above what they attribute (to Him).*

As shown in logic flowchart 14, the statement saying that we do not see contradiction in the creations and we do not see a major war in heaven is a fact. This indicates that the existence of more than one god is not possible, and therefore, there can only be one god. The opposite statement saying that we see contradiction in the creations and a war in the heavens is against the Law of Identity and is not logical.

When the final prophet, Muhammad PBUH, was asked about Almighty God, the answer came directly from Allah SWT in the holy Quran.

[112:1-4] *Say, 'He is God the One, God the eternal. He begot none nor was He begotten. No one is comparable to Him.*

In the above statement, Allah SWT describes clearly Himself to humanity that He is one and He is exalted above all His creatures.

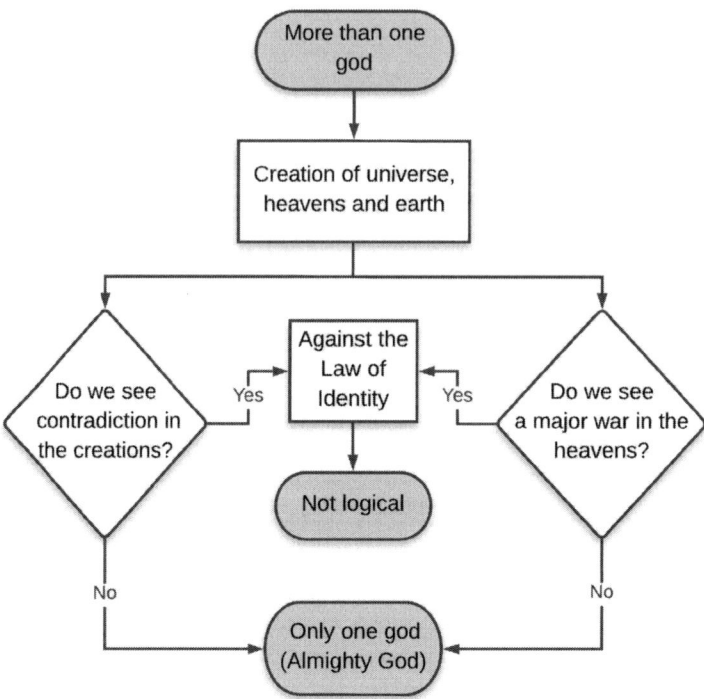

Logic flowchart 14: Only one god – Example 2

2 The creation

2.1 Why has Almighty God created life and humans?

Creation is fundamentally the consequence of the divine attribute of being the creator. Therefore, a creator who does not create is a contradiction in terms and definition. As the greatness of a writer becomes apparent in his writings, the perfection and completeness of Allah SWT is manifested in His creations.

To investigate the reason of our creation, we first need to know our position amongst all creatures and everything around us in this life. We are the only creatures on earth who have intellect and power over all other creatures. Allah SWT made us, all humans, the master of the heavens and earth, and made everything in heavens and earth subservient and beneficial to us.

[31:20] *Do you not see that Allah has made what is in the heavens and what is in the earth subservient to you.*

Allah SWT honoured us, the children of Adam, and made us the best of creatures that He has created, by giving us intellect and the freedom to choose between right and wrong, and good and evil.

[17:70] *And surely We have honoured the children of Adam, and We carry them in the land and the sea, and We have given them of the good things, and We have made them to excel by an appropriate excellence over most of those whom We have created.*

All plants, trees and palms on earth have been made available for our use.

[16:10-11] *He it is Who sends down water from the cloud for you; it gives drink, and by it (grow) the trees upon which you pasture. He causes to grow for you thereby herbage, and the olives, and the palm trees, and the grapes, and of all the fruits; most surely there is a sign in this for a people who give thought.*

Animals, both on earth and in sea, have also been made for our benefit. We can use them to produce food and clothing. Also, in the past, before the discovery of modern means of transportation, people used animals for transportation.

[16:5] *And cattle He has created for you (men): from them ye derive warmth, and numerous benefits, and of their (meat) ye eat.*

Sun, moon, starts and galaxies have been subservient for us. The sun and the moon are essential for us to survive on earth, and to count months and years. Stars and galaxies are used to show us directions, stabilise the universe and to be a sign for us to recognise the power of Almighty God.

[16:12] *And He has made subservient for you the night and the day and the sun and the moon, and the stars are made subservient by His commandment; most surely there are signs in this for a people who are wise.*

Even the whole universe has been created for us as a sign to remember Almighty God, to see how great He is and to think about Him. Allah SWT said this clearly in the holy Quran.

[3:190-191] *Most surely in the creation of the heavens and the earth and the alternation of the night and the day there are signs for men who understand. Those who remember Allah standing and sitting and lying on their sides and reflect on the creation of the heavens and the earth: Our Lord! Thou hast not created this in vain! Glory be to Thee; save us then from the chastisement of the fire.*

Thus, if everything in life and around us is created for us, for whom are we created? Everything around us is created for a sole purpose, which is to serve us, because we possess the highest intellect amongst all creatures. Therefore, for what purpose are we created and whom should we serve? The logical answer is that we are created to serve a creator who possesses a higher intellect than us, a super intellect, Almighty God. Therefore, the purpose of our creation is to serve the creator by establishing life on earth, recognising Him and worshipping Him.

As shown in logic flowchart 15, everything on earth is serving us as we possess the highest intellect. The statement saying that lower intellect serves higher intellect is a fact. Therefore, the statement saying that we should serve something having a lower intellect than us contradicts the original statement and is against the Law of Non-Contradiction.

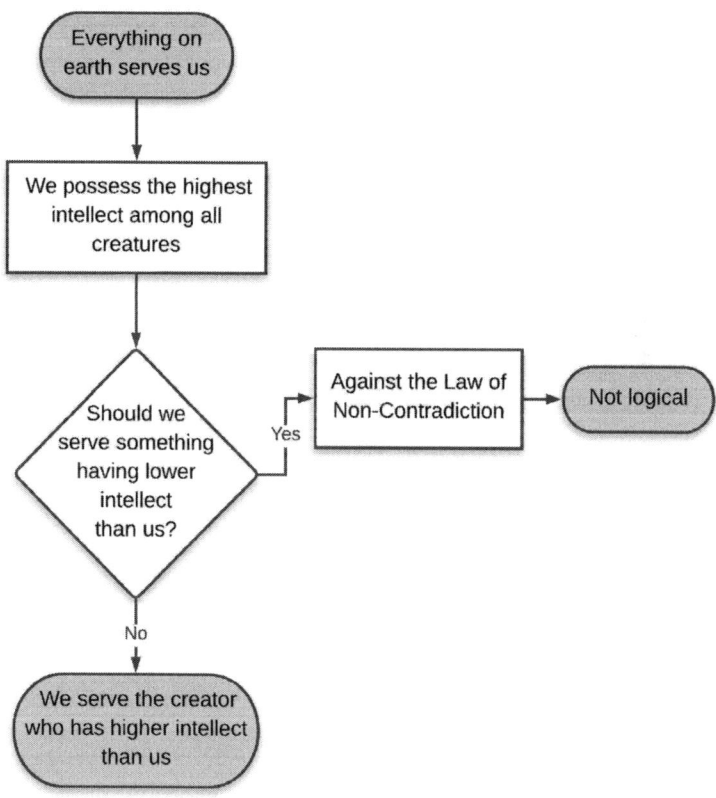

Logic flowchart 15: Creation of life – Example 1

We conclude that Almighty God has created this life and created us for a sole reason, that is, to recognise and worship Him. It is for the same reason that He created angels and jinns. Allah SWT said in the holy Quran:

[51:56] *I created the jinn and humankind only that they might worship Me.*

Scholars say that the word 'worship' in this verse indicates that humans and jinns first need to recognise Allah SWT, and then worship Him. This is because worshipping without recognising is not possible and does not make sense. Therefore, if humans recognise and know their creator, they will worship Him with different levels and degrees according to their knowledge.

But does Almighty God need us to recognise Him and worship Him? He is complete, self-sufficient and does not need anything from His creatures, so why did He create us and ask us to worship Him? Indeed, Allah SWT does not need us, but our creation is a part of His completeness. In other words, our creation demonstrates and confirms that Almighty God is complete and self-sufficient. Allah SWT has created the angels, who only worship Him, only obey Him and are not allowed to choose not to worship Him or disobey Him. As a part of His completeness, Allah SWT has also created the jinns, who are allowed to choose whether or not to worship Him, thus, to choose to obey or disobey Him.

Before the creation of Adam PBUH, the father of the jinns (called Iblis) chose to worship Allah SWT and he was so proud, his status became higher than the angels due to his choice. Iblis was called the Peacock of the angels because of his proudness.

Allah SWT created Adam PBUH with the same characteristics as the jinns, so He gave him the choice whether to worship Him. If Adam PBUH chose to worship Almighty God, his status would be higher than that of the angels, similar to the jinns. Moreover, Allah SWT gave Adam more knowledge and higher intellectual capabilities than angels and jinns. This can be clearly understood in the following dialogue between Almighty God and the angels in the holy Quran.

[2:30] *And when your Lord said to the angels, I am going to place in the earth a khalif (follower), they said: What! wilt Thou place in it such as shall make mischief in it and shed blood, and we celebrate Thy praise and extol Thy holiness? He said: Surely I know what you do not know.*

[2:31] *And He taught Adam all the names, then presented them to the angels; then He said: Tell me the names of those if you are right.*

[2:32] *They said: Glory be to Thee! we have no knowledge but that which Thou hast taught us; surely Thou art the Knowing, the Wise.*

[2:33] *He said: O Adam! Inform them of their names. Then when he had informed them of their names, He said: Did I not say to you that I surely know what is secret (unseen) in the heavens and the earth and (that) I know what you manifest and what you hide?*

Then, Almighty God asked the angels and Iblis to make obeisance to Adam PBUH. In other words, He asked them to admit that Adam PBUH is a better creature than them and that they accept to serve him. The angels obeyed Allah SWT and made obeisance to Adam PBUH, while Iblis disobeyed.

[2:34] *And when We said to the angels: Make obeisance to Adam they did obeisance, but Iblis (did it not). He refused and he was proud, and he was one of the unbelievers.*

In this way, the completeness of Almighty God is demonstrated, as Allah SWT created all possible types of creatures:
1. Creatures who worship Him and obey Him without having a choice, i.e. angels.
2. Creatures who choose whether to worship and obey Him, i.e. humans.

3. Creatures who choose not to worship Him and not to obey Him, i.e. devils.

This concept is illustrated in logic flowchart 16. The completeness of Almighty God is achieved by the creation of all types of creatures who have no choice but worship Him, creatures who have a choice whether to worship Him and creatures who choose to not worship Him.

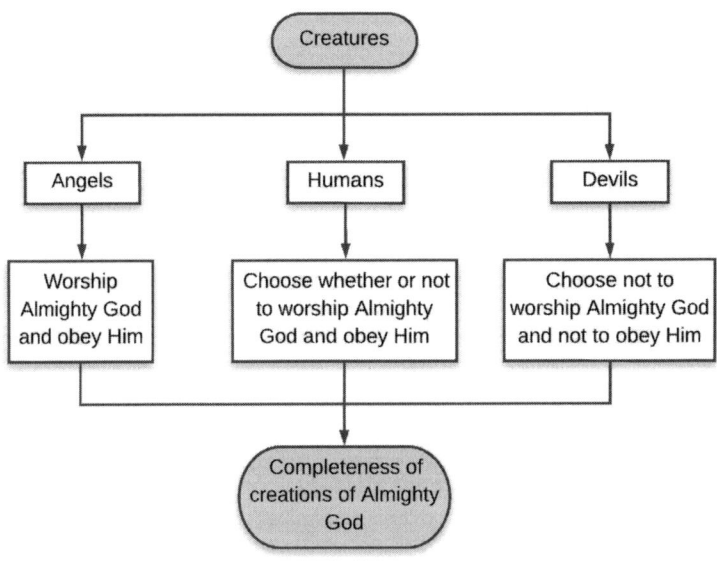

Logic flowchart 16: Creation of life – Example 2

For human beings, life becomes indeed like a test and a trial to see who will be able to recognise Almighty God, obey Him and do good deeds.

[67:1-2] *Blessed is He in Whose hand is the kingdom, and He has power over all things, who created death and life that He may try you, which of you is best in deeds; and He is the Mighty, the Forgiving.*

The creation of humans has been done in stages from the first human on earth, Adam PBUH, until the generation of people through reproduction. Allah SWT has created Adam PBUH from the dust of earth. Then, the dust was mixed with water and became wet clay.

[37:11] *Then ask them whether they are stronger in creation or those (others) whom We have created. Surely We created them of sticky clay.*

The clay became dry (sounding clay).

[15:26] *And certainly We created man of clay that gives forth sound, of black mud fashioned in shape.*

Then, Adam PBUH became human once the soul (spirit from Almighty God) is breathed into him.

[15:28-29] *Behold! thy Lord said to the angels: "I am about to create man, from sounding clay from mud moulded into shape; So when I have made him complete and breathed into him of My spirit, fall down making obeisance to him."*

In the above verse, Allah SWT mentioned that His spirit was breathed into sounding clay to give it life. This means that the creation of Adam's life was done by direct order from Allah SWT. This is similar to the creation of Jesus PBUH, with the exception that Adam PBUH had no father and no mother, but Jesus PBUH had a mother but no father.

[3:59] *Surely the likeness of Isa (Jesus) is with Allah as the likeness of Adam; He created him from dust, then said to him, Be, and he was.*

Then, the last stage in the creation of humans, the son of Adam, is through reproduction so that life will continue on earth until the day of judgement. The whole process of creating a baby in the womb of his mother is described by Almighty God in the holy Quran.

[23:12] *And certainly We created man of an extract of clay, Then We made him a small seed in a firm resting-place, Then We made the seed a clot, then We made the clot a lump of flesh, then We made (in) the lump of flesh bones, then We clothed the bones with flesh, then We caused it to grow into another creation, so blessed be Allah, the best of the creators.*

The creation of Adam PBUH without a father or a mother is a miracle similar to the creation of Jesus from a mother and without a father. Furthermore, the soul of the first human female, Eva, is created from Adam PBUH as mentioned by Allah SWT in the holy Quran.

[4:1] *O mankind! Be careful of your duty to your Lord Who created you from a single soul and from it created its mate and from them twain hath spread abroad a multitude of men and women. Be careful of your duty toward Allah in Whom ye claim (your rights) of one another, and toward the wombs (that bare you). Lo! Allah hath been a watcher over you.*

In this way the completeness of Almighty God is demonstrated by creating humans in all possible ways as illustrated in logic flowchart 17.
1. Adam PBUH is created without a male and without a female.
2. Eva is created from a male and without a female.
3. Jesus PBUH is created from a female, without a male.
4. All humans are created from a male and a female.

The relationship between this life and the hereafter, eternal life after death, can be compared to the relationship between a baby's life in the womb and this worldly life. A baby in the mother's womb goes through different developmental stages over a period of seven to nine months. Every moment and every day, he grows up and his development continues until the moment comes for him to leave the womb and enter this world. Similarly, we also live and go through different developmental stages during a life of approximately 70-100 years. At some point, we will also have to leave this world and move to another world.

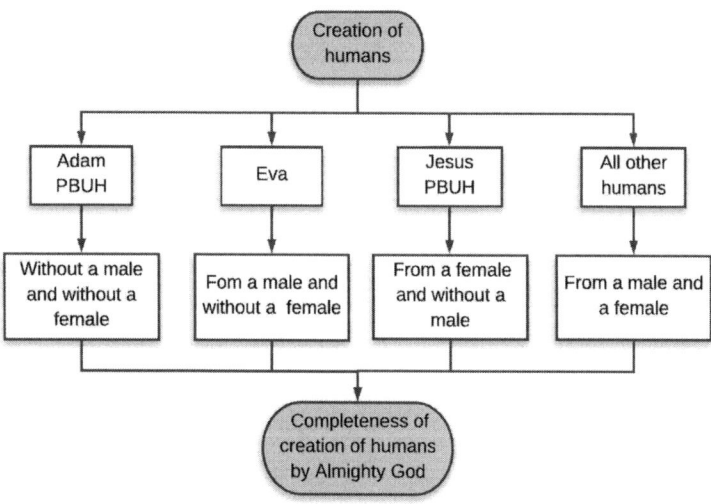

Logic flowchart 17: Creation of life – Example 3

Although the human's body keeps developing from the early days in the womb until the last day on earth, the spirit stays the same and does not change. The moment when the baby leaves the womb is in fact a death moment for him as he is leaving one world for another. Similarly, the death moment in this life is defined as leaving one world for another.

As illustrated in logic flowchart 18, the statement saying that the spirit of life in the womb is the same as that in this worldly life is a fact. Therefore, the statement saying that it is not the same is against the Law of Identity. As the spirit is the same in the first two lives, the statement saying that it is also the same in the hereafter should be true. Thus, the opposite statement is against the Law of Non-Contradiction.

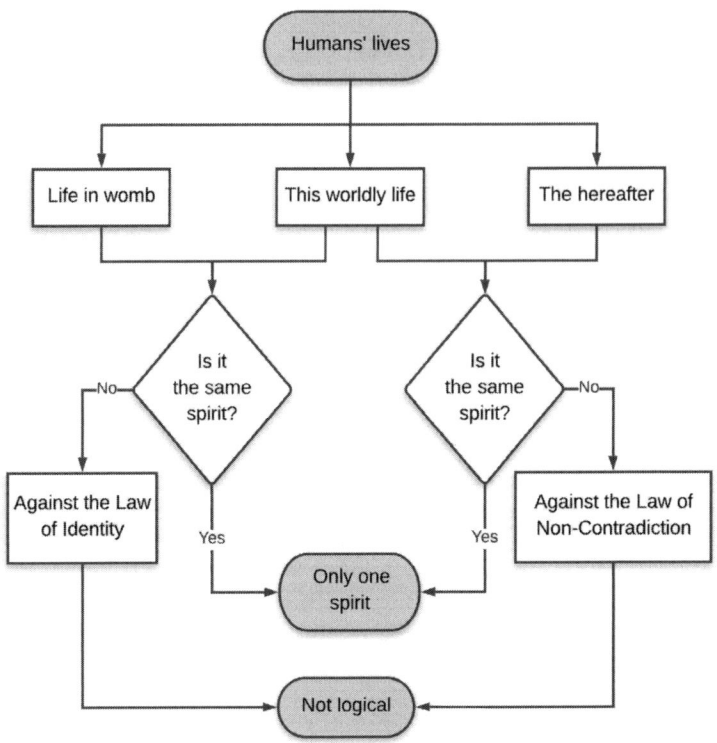

Logic flowchart 18: Creation of life – Example 4

In fact, we are not created for this worldly life, but we are created to return to Almighty God and to eternally live in the hereafter. It is not possible to assume that we are created with no purpose and that our presence on earth has no meaning or is not important. In the holy Quran, Allah SWT mentions clearly that this is not possible as it is against His great wisdom.

[23:115-116] *What! did you then think that We had created you in vain and that you shall not be returned to Us? So exalted be Allah, the True King; no god is there but He, the Lord of the honourable dominion.*

Allah SWT creates us because He loves us. He creates us for happiness and eternity in the hereafter and gives us this worldly life as a unique chance to recognise Him through seeking knowledge and using our intellect. In the hereafter, recognising Almighty God will be inherently similar to the case of angels. As mentioned by our prophet Mohammed PBUH, the sign of love from Allah SWT for a certain person can be seen in how much this person remembers Allah SWT.

As we are created to serve and worship Almighty God, why is evil created? Would not life be better with only good and without any evil? What is the importance of the existence of evil? Why has Almighty God created evil? In the next section, we provide answers to these questions.

2.2 Why has Almighty God created evil?

Firstly, we have to clarify that Allah SWT has created evil, but He did not allow people to do it. In contrast, He asked them to do good deeds and to avoid doing evil deeds:

[7:28-29] *Say: Surely Allah does not enjoin evil; do you say against Allah what you do not know? Say: My Lord has enjoined justice.*

Thus, Almighty God forbids evil and enjoins justice, love, forgiveness and mercy, so why does He permit wrongdoing, such as killing or stealing? Simply, because He has created us with the freedom to choose what we do, and He has given us the freedom to do either good or evil. This is, in fact, a part of the test in this worldly life. Freedom means that mistakes can be made and this is, indeed, an essential part of freedom. Allah SWT could take away our freedom and enforce us to obey Him, but in such a case we would be like angels and life would have no meaning.

The creation of evil is part of the test that Allah SWT has created for human beings, which is to choose between good and evil. If there was no evil, there would be no test, we would be like angels and life would be meaningless. The test from Almighty God in this life classifies people in grades in the hereafter and defines their positions in the next life when we return to Him.

[21:35] *Every soul must taste of death and We try you by evil and good by way of probation; and to Us you shall be brought back.*

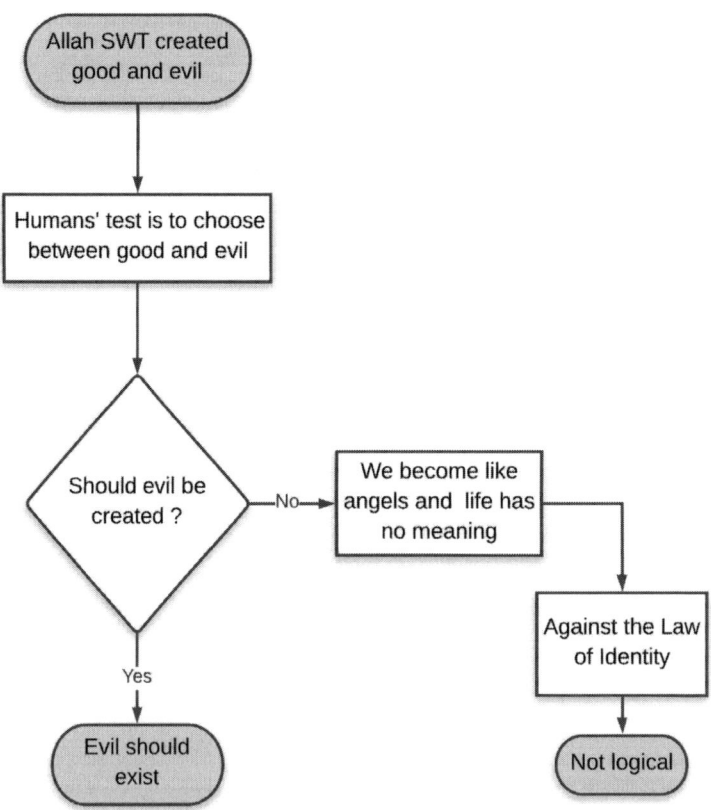

Logic flowchart 19: Creation of evil – Example 1

As illustrated in logic flowchart 19, if humans' test is to choose between good and evil, then the statement saying that evil should exist is a fact. Doing only good is not a characteristic of humans but rather a characteristic of angels. In such a case, the humans' test is not possible and life loses its meaning. Therefore, the statement saying that evil should not exist is against the Law of Identity.

Some people may recognise and worship Almighty God in good circumstances and others may recognise and worship Him in difficult circumstances. The successful person is who recognises Allah SWT in both circumstances. Therefore, the creation of both good and evil is essential for the humans' test, which is required to distinguish between believers and nonbelievers.

[29:2-3] *Do men think that they will be left alone on saying, We believe, and not be tried? And certainly We tried those before them, so Allah will certainly know those who are true and He will certainly know the liars.*

With a deep and fair looking at the world around us, we will discover that good is the general rule and evil is the exceptional case. For example, being healthy is the general rule and getting sick is the exceptional case. The majority of us stay most of our lives in a healthy state and become sick only occasionally. Similarly, the duration of earthquakes is only a few minutes, which is short compared to the billions of years of earth life. Also, the duration of wars is considered short compared to the long duration of peace on earth.

Good occupies the biggest part of life, while evil occupies a small part of it. Thus, good will never be complete or in its correct shape without evil. Similarly, life will not be complete or end without death. Without death or evil, this life would be a paradise, which it is not intended to be because Almighty God has created it as a temporary life, not as a permanent eternal life. Thus, death has been created to limit this worldly life and to make it temporary. In contrast, Almighty God has created paradise to be the permanent life in the hereafter. Therefore, there will be neither death nor evil in paradise.

A comparison between this worldly life and paradise is illustrated in logic flowchart 20. As death and evil exist in this worldly life, the statement saying that this worldly life is temporary is a fact. Consequently, the statement saying that this worldly life is permanent is against the Law of Identity. Similarly, as death and evil do not exist in paradise, the statement saying that life in paradise is permanent is a fact. Consequently, the statement saying that life in paradise is temporary is against the Law of Identity.

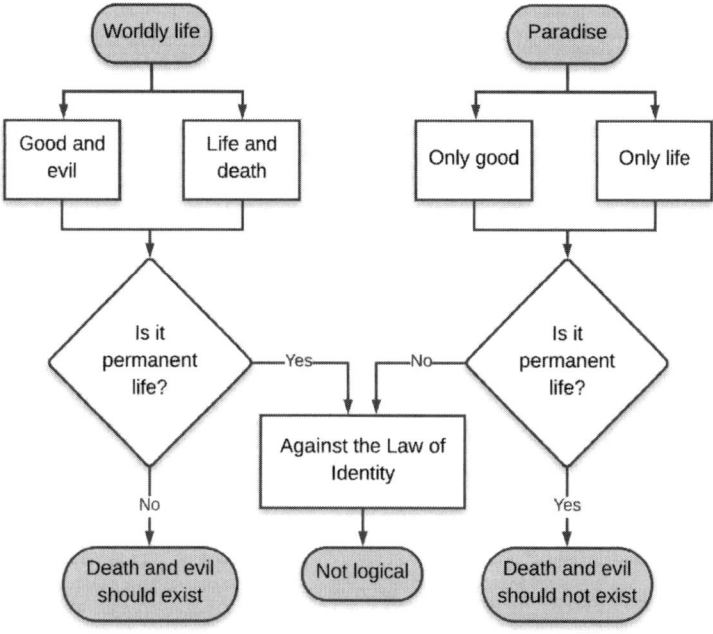

Logic flowchart 20: Creation of evil – Example 2

Furthermore, we can see some good consequences from the evils that Allah SWT has created. Illness leads to prevention, pain creates hardness and resistance, and earthquakes release the pressure from inside the earth. Although wars are evil, they lead to union of nations and new inventions. Seven wartime inventions were produced during wars and we use them every day, namely canned food, plastic surgery, sanitary napkins, duct tape, microwave ovens, digital photography and internet.

Evil is an essential part of our worldly life to make it complete. How would we know the importance of good, if evil did not exist? How would we know the importance of health, if there was no illness? How would we know the importance of peace if there were no wars? How would we know beauty, if there was no ugliness? How would we know normality if there was no oddity? Therefore, evil complements good and is essential for this life.

As illustrated in logic flowchart 21, if evil does not exist, we would not be able to know the importance of good. According to the original statement, we are able to know the importance of good with the existence of evil. So, the statement saying that

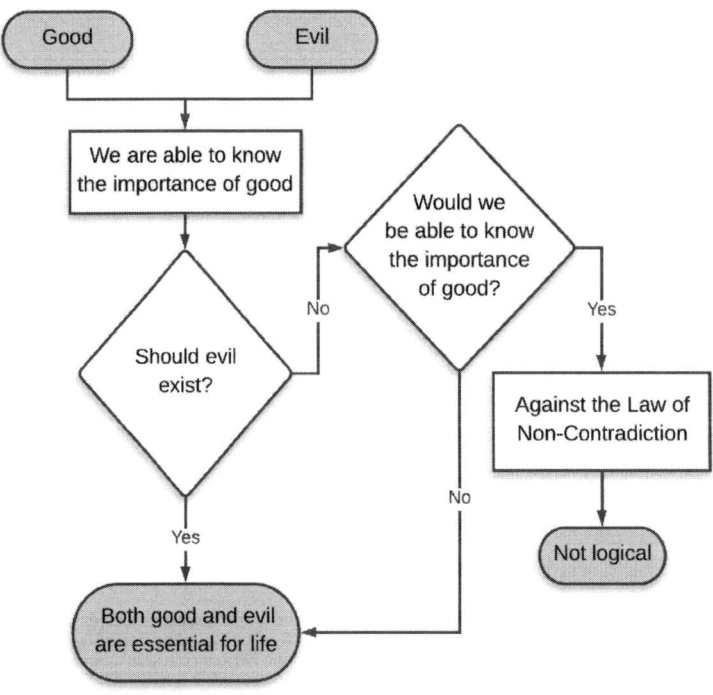

Logic flowchart 21: Creation of evil – Example 3

we would be able to know the importance of good without evil is against the Low of Non-Contradiction.

The existence of evil also demonstrates the completeness of Almighty God. He created everything and its opposite to complete the creation. He created day and night, male and female, light and darkness, love and hate, health and illness, life and death, happiness and sadness, and good and evil. As Allah SWT is able to create good and makes use of it as He wishes, He should also be able to create evil and make use of it as He wishes. This concept is illustrated in logic flowchart 22. Asking Allah SWT for giving us good and protect us from evil can also be seen as completeness in worshipping Him.

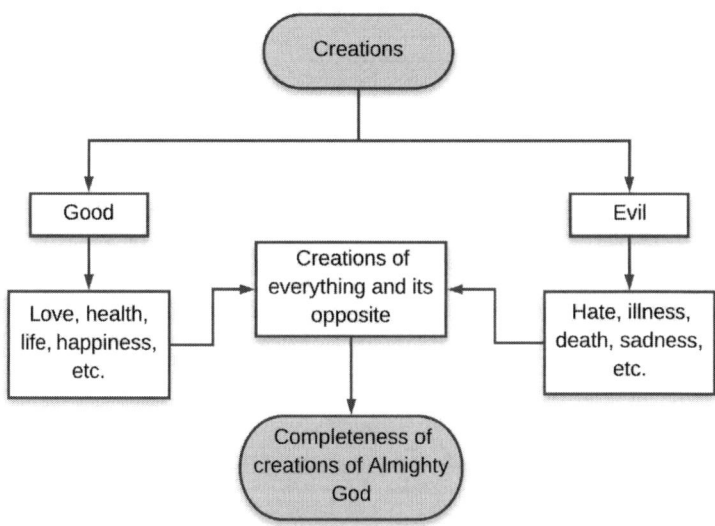

Logic flowchart 22: Creation of evil – Example 4

This life is just a part of the whole story, which will continue after death. We cannot base our judgement on one part of the story and not consider the remaining parts as this kind of judgement would not be complete. It is not possible to have a life without illness, pain or death. Otherwise, as mentioned earlier, we would be in paradise, which will only be a future part of the story.

2.3 Can science create?

Science does not create but rather it explains existing laws. Isaac Newton discovered the law of gravity, but he did not create gravity. Likewise, Albert Einstein discovered the relativity, but he did not create anything related to his theory, e.g. space and time. Therefore, science answers the question 'what is this?', but it does not answer the question 'why does this exist?' or 'who made this?'

A real creation, i.e. something made from nothing, without materials, substances, machines or equipment, is unique to Almighty God alone. Although humans may claim that they can create, in fact, they make, manufacture and fabricate, but they do not create. People merely manipulate and imitate what already exists, i.e. what was already created by Allah SWT and found in nature. For example, a table is made from wood coming from trees and held together with nails and screws made from metal. Therefore, a carpenter has manufactured it, but we cannot say that he created it because he had to use materials coming from earth and equipment.

Therefore, humans manufacture things but they do not create them, as most of these things can be traced back to basic elements, which humans have found on earth. Even an artist makes designs based on what he has seen in nature and around him. He cannot imagine what has not been perceived by his senses. Thus, all of the artist's thoughts are reflections of what was already created on earth and in heavens.

Only Almighty God alone creates from nothing as He creates the universe from nothing. Scientists agreed that the universe started according to the big-bang theory about 14 billion years ago. They also agreed that at that moment of time, the entire observable universe was an infinitesimally tiny substance and could be estimated as roughly a million billion billion times smaller than a single atom. This infinitesimally tiny substance is also described as singularity, which means that the substance was infinitely small and infinitely dense. In other words, there was almost nothing.

A comparison between the creation of the universe, heaven and earth by Almighty God and man-made structures and machines, is illustrated in logic flowchart 23. The statement saying that materials and equipment are required to make structures is a fact. Therefore, the statement saying that they are not required is against the Law of Identity. Similarly, the statement saying that

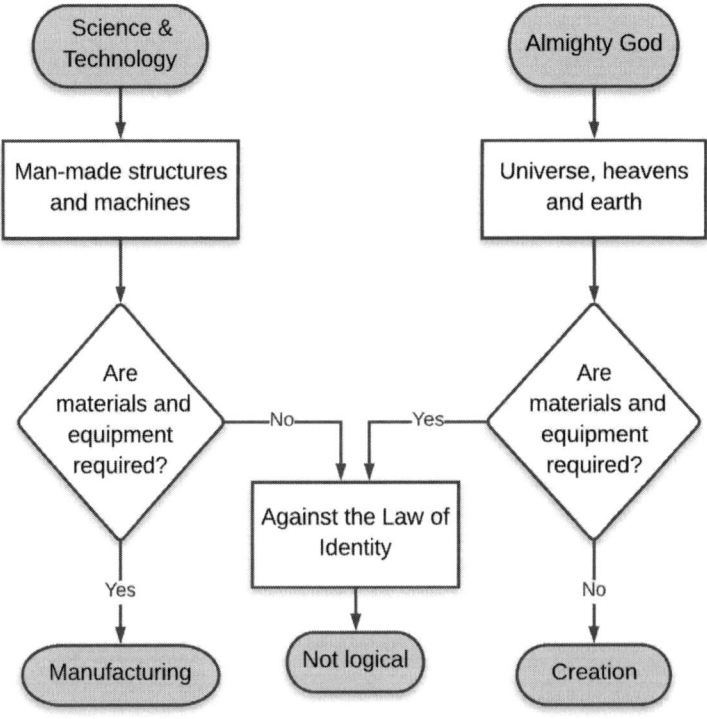

Logic flowchart 23: Science does not create – Example 1

materials and equipment are not required for the creation of the universe, heavens or earth (according to the big-bang theory) is a fact. Therefore, the statement saying that they are required is against the Law of Identity.

In fact, no comparison can be made between the creations of Almighty God and the human-made things. Allah SWT denies any such comparisons, as it would give Him human limitations.

[42:11] *There is nothing like Him and He is hearer and seer of all.*

Allah SWT describes Himself in many verses in the holy Quran as the creator in order to emphasise that everything is created by Him and belongs to only Him.

[39:62] *God created all things and He is the agent on which all things depend.*

[37:96] *And God created you all and whatever you do.*

Any scientist carrying out tests in chemical labs or doing genetic engineering makes use of substances and equipment, and therefore, what he produces, is not a creation but rather the making and imitation of nature created by Allah SWT. Producing a living organism from non-living organisms still cannot be called creation of life because of the need for materials. For example, the production of an organic compound (e.g. urea) from an inorganic compound (e.g. ammonium cyanate), which is known as Wöhler synthesis, is no more than a fabrication experiment of an organism. The experiment needs chemical solutions, such as potassium cyanate and ammonium chloride, and heating and cooling equipment, i.e. a specific environment.

Similarly, an artificial cell is made of polymers, crosslinked proteins and lipid membranes. Besides, laboratory equipment, high-pressure homogenisers, micro-fluidisers or emulsion mixing machines, are required to perform the experiment. Making synthetic DNA requires raw materials such as taq DNA polymerase, primers, nucleotides and buffer solution. It should also be processed using programming codes, computers and other devices.

The three examples mentioned above are illustrated in logic flowchart 24. As all three living things require raw materials as well as equipment, they cannot be classified as created things. The process of making them can be rather described as fabrication or imitation using already-existing materials.

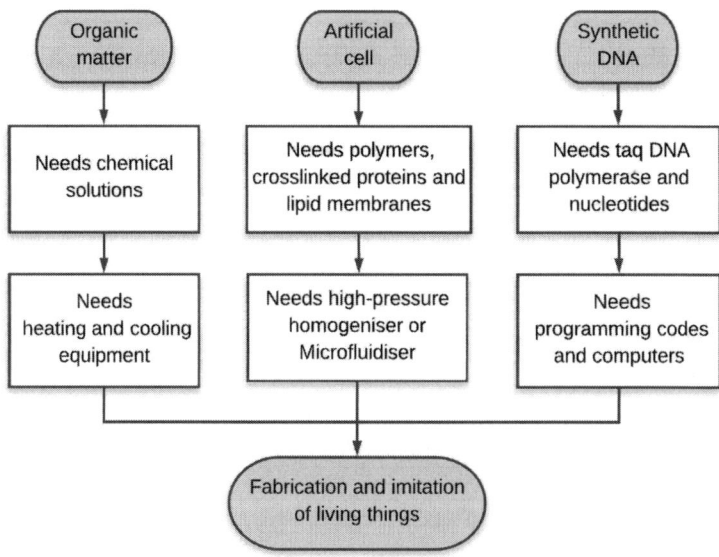

Logic flowchart 24: Science does not create – Example 2

Although life may be defined scientifically by living organisms, this definition is not the kind of life meant by creation. The definition of life, in the sense of creation, is the condition distinguishing human beings and animals from non-organic things. This condition includes the ability to reproduce, the capacity to grow and the termination to death. Therefore, creation of life is mainly related to human beings and animals. Real creation of humans, animals, birds and insects is to make the physical body from dust of the ground and breathe into the body so that it becomes alive.

[3:49] *And (make him) a messenger to the children of Israel: That I have come to you with a sign from your Lord, that I determine for you out of dust like the form of a bird, then I breathe into it and it becomes a bird with Allah's permission.*

Allah SWT created the heavens, earth and everything between them, including humans, animals, plants and mountains. He challenges the nonbelievers to create anything similar to His creations.

[31:11] *This is Allah's creation, but show Me what those besides Him have created. Nay, the unjust are in manifest error.*

Science will never be able to create a human being, an animal or even an insect. Allah SWT challenges all mankind to create a fly or an insect.

[22:73] *O people! a parable is set forth, therefore listen to it: surely those whom you call upon besides Allah cannot create fly (or an insect), though they should all gather for it, and should the fly snatch away anything from them, they could not take it back from it, weak are the invoker and the invoked.*

As illustrated in logic flowchart 25 and explained in the next chapter, human beings consist of a body and a spirit or soul. As science can create neither the physical body nor the spirit, the statement saying that science cannot create them is a fact. Therefore, the statement saying that science can create them is against the Law of Identity and leads to an illogical conclusion.

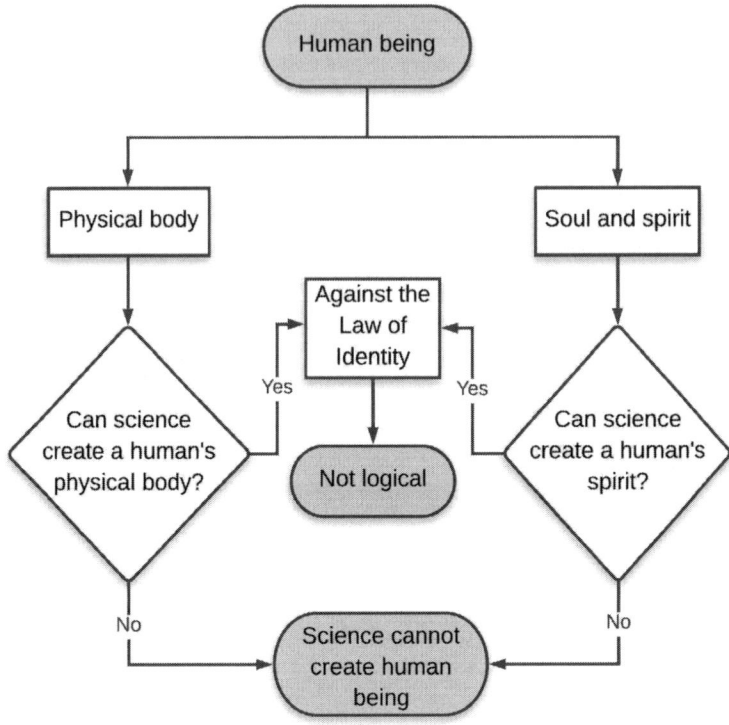

Logic flowchart 25: Science does not create – Example 3

In fact, science proves the existence of a great creator, Almighty God. It is well known that in science and mathematics, no greater being could be imagined. However, if Almighty God did not exist, then a greater being had to be possible to imagine, i.e. one which exists. Since it is not possible, by definition, to imagine a greater being than the greatest being imaginable, Almighty God has to exist. Almighty God is then defined as the greatest being in the universe. As illustrated in logic flowchart 26, the statement saying that a greater being could not be imagined is a fact. Therefore, the statement saying that a greater being could be imagined is against the Law of Identity.

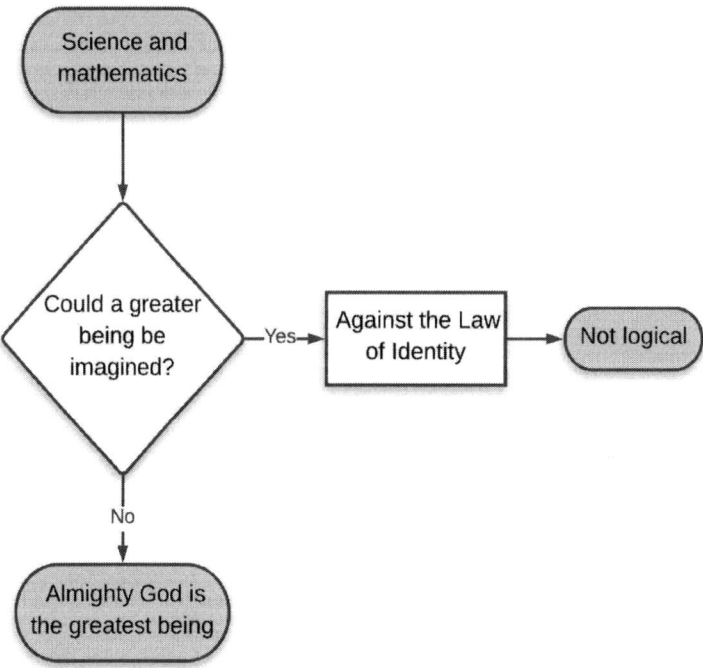

Logic flowchart 26: Science does not create – Example 4

3 The soul

3.1 What is the difference between the soul and the spirit?

First we have to clarify that, as Almighty God said in the holy Quran, human beings do not have the knowledge of the soul or the spirit.

[17:85] *And they ask you about the soul. Say: The soul is one of the commands of my Lord, and you are not given aught of knowledge but a little.*

The difference between the soul and the spirit is not in the identity, but rather in the characteristic. This means that the soul and the spirit are the same thing or have the same identity. However, the word soul is used when it is inside the human body, but the word spirit is used when it is outside the human body. For example, during our worldly life, it is called a soul and after death it becomes a spirit.

In the holy Quran, the soul is mentioned to refer to mankind in this worldly life.

[59:18] *O you who believe! Be careful of (your duty to) Allah, and let every soul consider what it has sent on for the morrow (near future), and be careful of (your duty to) Allah; surely Allah is Aware of what you do.*

[59:19] *And be not like those who forsook Allah, so He made them forsake their own souls: these it is that are the transgressors.*

The soul is also mentioned in the day of judgement and the hereafter, which indicate that both physical body and spirit will be in the next life.

[2:281] *And guard yourselves against a day in which you shall be returned to Allah; then every soul shall be paid back in full what it has earned, and they shall not be dealt with unjustly.*

[82:19] *The day on which no soul shall control anything for (another) soul; and the command on that day shall be entirely Allah's.*

[41:31] *We are your guardians in this world's life and in the hereafter, and you shall have therein what your souls desire and you shall have therein what you ask for.*

However, the human spirit is mentioned when it is not yet blown into the physical body.

[32:9] *Then He made him complete and breathed into him of His spirit, and made for you the ears and the eyes and the hearts; little is it that you give thanks.*

[38:72] *So when I have made him complete and breathed into him of My spirit, then fall down making obeisance to him.*

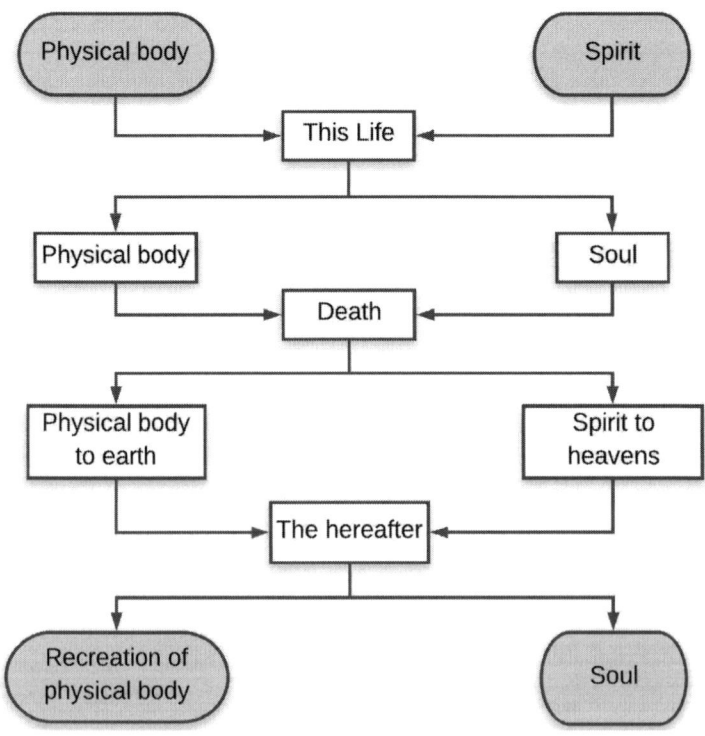

Logic flowchart 27: The soul – Example 1

As shown in logic flowchart 27, the physical body and the spirit are defined as separate identities. When the spirit is blown into the physical body, i.e. baby in womb, it becomes a soul. At death, when the soul is separated from the physical body, it becomes a spirit again. After death, the physical body goes to ground and becomes dust, while the spirit returns to its creator in the heavens and stays in its eternal life. In the next life, the physical body will be recreated and the spirit becomes a soul again.

We explained above the difference between the soul and the spirit, but does the soul or the spirit exist? What is the logical proof that the soul exists? Is the soul limited in time and space? What is the need for a spiritual part for human beings? We provide answers to these questions in the next section.

3.2 Does the soul exist?

The soul is something non-physical. A proof of existence of the soul in the physical body can be seen in different aspects, such as a) the mysteries of birth and death, b) the play of consciousness during dreams and c) the commonest mental operations, such as imagination and memory. These three aspects suggest that a vital life force exists independent of the physical body, which is the soul. For example, how do we live our dreams while sleeping? With our physical body or with something else? It is impossible to say that we dream with our physical body, so it should be with something else, which is again the soul.

This concept is illustrated in logic flowchart 28. The statement saying that the three aspects described above cannot depend only on the physical body is a fact. Therefore, the statement saying that they depend only on the physical body is not logical and is against the Law of Identity.

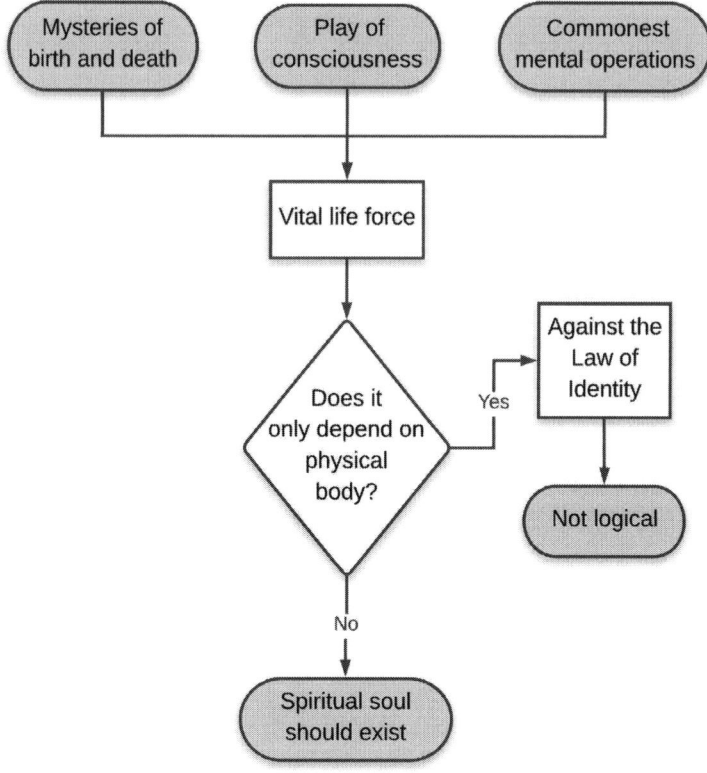

Logic flowchart 28: The soul – Example 2

As spirit is not a physical quantity, scientific experiments cannot prove when the soul is outside the body, i.e. spirit after death. However, it can be experimentally proven by other sciences, such as parapsychology or mediumship, i.e. mediate communication between spirits of the dead and souls of living human beings.

A second proof of the existence of the soul is explained as follows. Human beings have two different natures or parts. The first one is the body, which is the outer physical part. It has all physical characteristics, such as weight, dimensions, measures, and is restricted to space and time. It can change from one situation to another, i.e. health to ill, fat to thin, active to lazy, and wake to sleep.

The second nature is inside the human and is completely different from the first one. This second nature is not restricted to space or time and is related to the mind and conscience of humans. It is a feeling that does not change in time and it continues without stopping. The nature of this second part is spiritual. We feel that we are getting old through the outer physical body, but we do not feel our age inside ourselves because, as we pass through different stages in our lives, we see ourselves in all these stages, i.e. childhood, adulthood and midlife. Therefore, the inner spiritual part is not restricted to space and time, and it does not feel age.

This concept is illustrated in logic flowchart 29. The statement saying that the physical part of human nature is restricted to

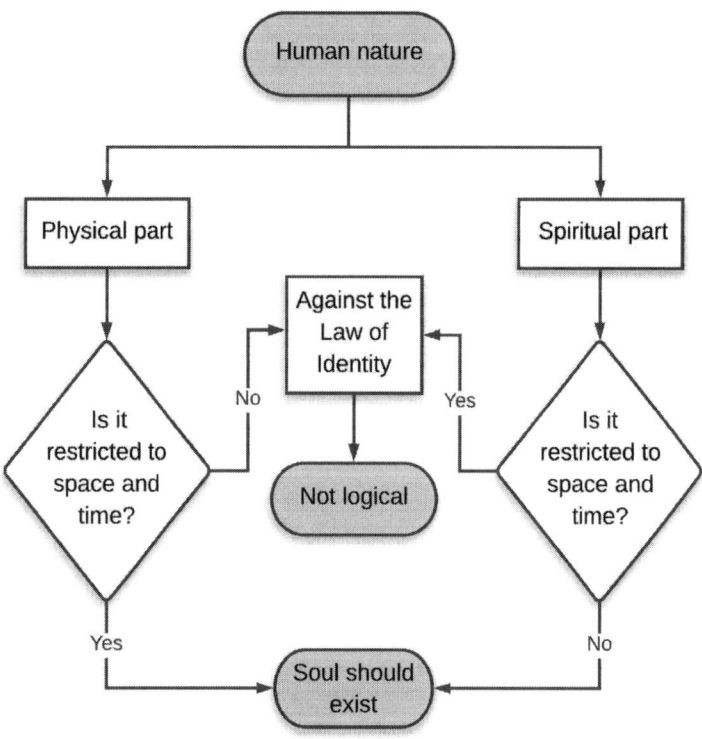

Logic flowchart 29: The soul – Example 3

space and time is a fact. Similarly, the statement saying that the spiritual part of human nature is not restricted to space and time is also a fact. Therefore, the opposite statements are against the Law of Identity and the soul should exist.

Another proof of the existence of the spiritual soul is based on the relativity of motion. We cannot see motion unless we are outside of it. For example, we can see the motion of the sun and the moon because we are outside of them. But we cannot see or feel the motion of the earth because we are part of it and we move with it. We can only feel the motion of the earth when we look at the heavens, i.e. the sun, the moon and the stars. Similarly, when we are in a train or a car, we only feel the motion when we look at exterior fixed objects or another object that moves at a different speed. The observer in a fixed position will obviously see this motion. Therefore, we cannot see or feel the motion unless there is a relative motion between two objects.

Similarly, our physical part cannot feel time or see its effect unless there is another part that is fixed in time and not affected by time. In other words, there should be an observer that watches the physical body to realise its motion with time. This observer is the spiritual soul. This means that there is a part of us, the spiritual soul, that is outside time, in order to be able to observe time. Therefore, this part is eternal, is not affected by time and does not get old.

A comparison between a train or car and the physical human body is shown in logic flowchart 30. The statement saying that we cannot feel the absolute motion of a train or a car without a fixed observer is a fact. Therefore, the statement saying that we can feel its absolute motion without a fixed observer is against the Law of Identify. Similarly, the statement saying that we cannot feel the age of our physical bodies without a fixed observer is a fact. Therefore, the statement saying that we can feel the age of our physical bodies without a fixed observer is against the Law of Identify. The fixed observer in this case is the soul, which should be independent of age and time.

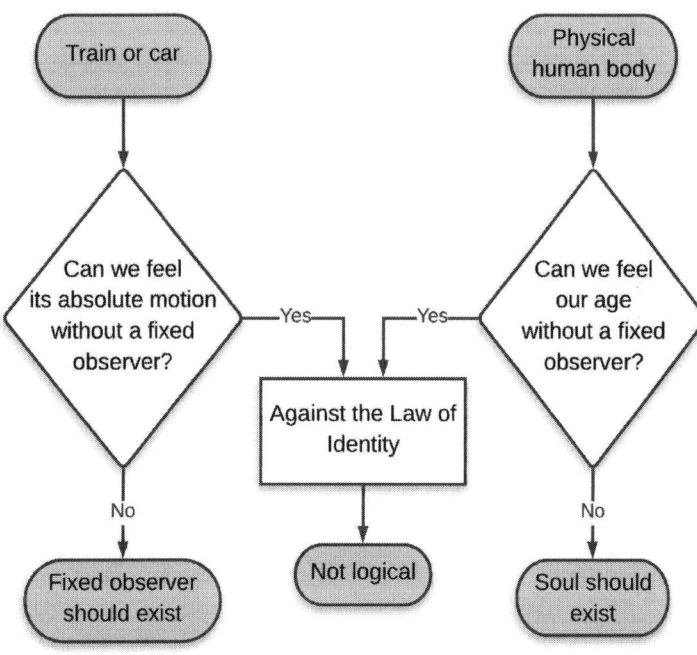

Logic flowchart 30: The soul – Example 4

If we agree that a human has two natures – a physical body and a spiritual soul – which one controls the other? Which one follows the other? Does the outer body control the inner soul or does the inner soul control the outer body? When we decide to fast, the outer body is hungry and wants to eat, but the inner soul decides not to eat. When we wake up in the morning, the inner soul starts to plan the day and the outer body follows the plan during the day. In time of war, a soldier may decide to sacrifice his outer body by the command from his inner soul.

The brain is a part of the physical body and is not a part of the soul. Like cells in the physical body, the brain receives commands from the soul and transfers them to the remaining parts of the body to take actions. Therefore, the brain is of a physical and not a spiritual nature. It can be regarded as a mediator between the physical body and the soul.

Hence we can conclude that the primary part of humans is the spiritual soul, while the secondary part is the physical body. At the time of death, the secondary part starts to diminish and becomes dust, whereas the primary part remains and joins its spiritual life by Almighty God.

As logic flowchart 31 illustrates, the statement saying that the spiritual soul controls the physical body is a fact. Therefore, the statement saying that the spiritual soul does not control the physical body is against the Law of Identity. The spiritual soul should then be the essential part of the human nature.

As Muslims, we believe, that after death, resurrection will take place for the day of judgement and the hereafter. So what is the logical reasoning behind the resurrection? We observe that everything around us has a start and an end, and then a restart, continuing the cycle. After daylight comes night and then again daylight. Equally, the sun, the moon and the stars come and go, and then come back in cycles. We sleep, wake up, sleep again, and so on, in cycles. Therefore, we live and we will die, and it is logic to assume that we will revive because the soul is eternal.

[39:42] *Allah takes the souls at the time of their death, and those that die not during their sleep; then He withholds those on whom He has passed the decree of death and sends the others back till an appointed term; most surely there are signs in this for a people who reflect.*

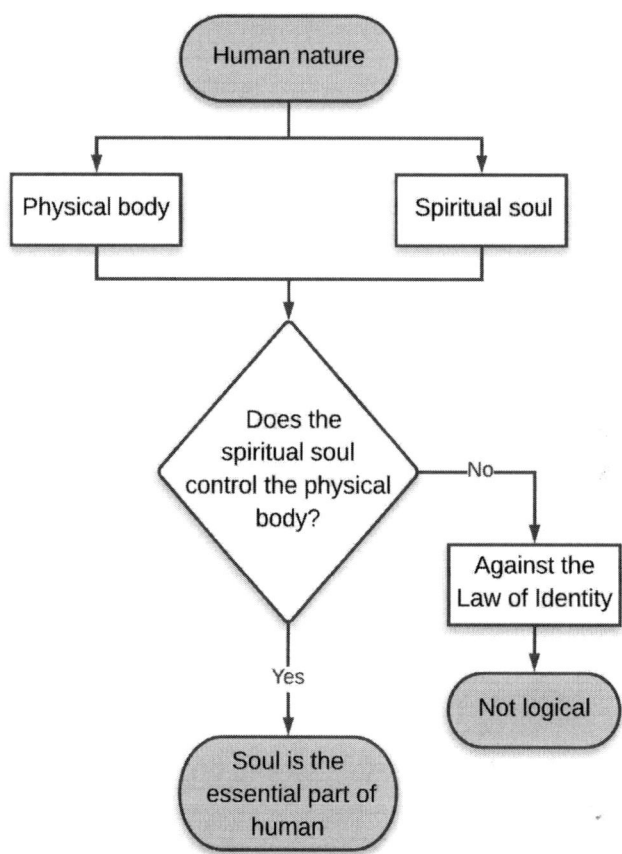

Logic flowchart 31: The soul – Example 5

4 The hereafter

4.1 What is proof of the hereafter?

Belief in the next life – the hereafter – is an important part of the belief in Almighty God. It means that we believe that there will be a life after death and that this next life is eternal and forever. Almighty God will collapse this current universe to reconstruct a new universe that will live forever.

[21:104] *On the day when We will roll up heaven like the rolling up of the scroll for writings, as We originated the first creation, (so) We shall reproduce it; a promise (binding on Us); surely We will bring it about.*

The concept of a next life requires that our current universe and humans on earth will vanish in time. Scientifically speaking, and without any doubt, this world will vanish in time and all humans will die at some stage. No one can argue that eternity on this earth is impossible.

Scientists who do not want to believe in the hereafter try to investigate the reasons for death in order to find a way to prevent it. However, they face a great failure and all their studies and research always conclude that there is no way to prevent death and that it is impossible to have eternity on earth. There are lots of reasons for death and none of them can be prevented.

Death can be caused by old age, diseases, including Aids and cancer, heart attacks, accidents or suicide, and is not related to a specific age. Babies, children, young people, as well as older people may die at any time and for any reason. No one can find a way to prevent death from happening or to save himself from death. With the advancement of medicine and technology, it might be possible to prolong life with a few years, but it is impossible to keep it forever.

Death is a separation between the physical body and spiritual soul of a human. The physical body vanishes and will be recreated by Almighty God, while the spiritual soul stays forever without changes. An example of this process can be seen in our worldly life journey. We know that the human body contains approximately 37.2 trillion cells. Human cells are dying and being replaced all the time so that in a period of 7 to 15 years, almost all cells are replaced. Thus, the outer physical body is completely recreated. However, the inner spiritual soul remains unchanged, as humans retain their knowledge, ideas, concepts, style, etc. Right through life, a human feels like the same person.

If we completely vanish after death, our feelings would be changed when all our cells (physical body) have been recreated, but we all know that this is not the case. This confirms that humans not only have a physical body, but there is something else that does not change and is not affected by the changes in the body. Thus, when the physical body dies, we do not vanish because, although our bodies die several times during our lives, we remain alive.

As illustrated in logic flowchart 32, the statement saying that humans' spiritual soul does not change after the replacement of all the physical body's cells is a fact. Therefore, the statement saying that humans' spiritual soul changes after the replacement of all the physical body's cells is against the Law of Identity and is not logical. Furthermore, if the physical body died and was recreated several times during our worldly life, it is logically possible that it would be recreated after death with the soul remaining unchanged.

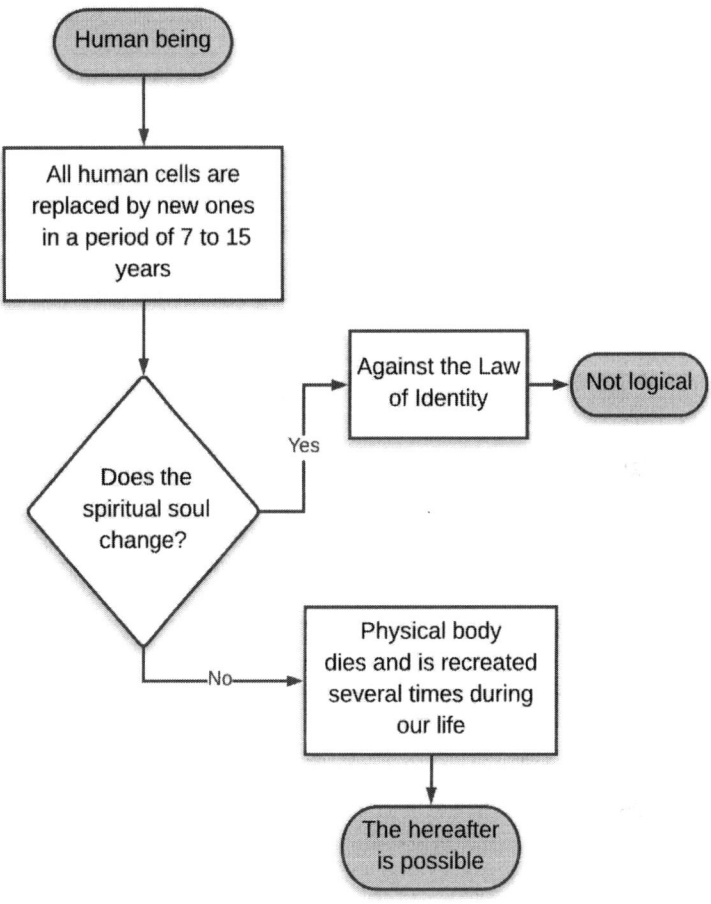

Logic flowchart 32: The proof of the hereafter – Example 1

Another logical proof of the hereafter is the need for justice. In other words, people have a need to judge each other and evaluate each other's deeds. For example, not all crimes committed on earth are being judged by the authorities. This is also the case when criminals themselves are the people who control the authorities, so they steal, cheat and commit crimes against other people without any judgement. Similarly, the transgression of a powerful man against a weak man or the transgression of a powerful country against a weak country cannot be judged on this earth. In the first chapter, we have proven that Allah SWT exits, so He should be the most just and He will never allow injustice to take place on earth without final judgement.

[4:40] *Surely Allah does not do injustice to the weight of an atom, and if it is a good deed He multiplies it and gives from Himself a great reward.*

Many criminals commit several crimes in their lives and they die without judgement or punishment. Should they ever be judged or punished? Common sense says, 'yes, they should be judged and they should be punished for their crimes against other people'. There is no other way to get this judgement, except in the hereafter. Therefore, the hereafter has to exist. Without life after death, this worldly life cannot be justified.

[3:185] *Every soul shall taste of death, and you shall only be paid fully your reward on the resurrection day; then whoever is removed far away from the fire and is made to enter the garden he indeed has attained the object; and the life of this world is nothing but a provision of vanities.*

As logic flowchart 33 illustrates, the statement saying that all criminals in this life are not judged or punished is a fact. Therefore, the opposite statement saying that all criminals in this life are judged and punished is against the Law of Identity. The hereafter should exist in order to punish the criminals and complete justice, which is incomplete in this worldly life.

Many war criminals who commit crimes against humanity and kill thousands and millions of people throughout history are not punished. Even if they were punished by the maximum possible punishment in this life – the death penalty – this punishment would not be just because one death does not compensate for the millions of people killed at the hands of war criminals. Therefore, it would be logic to say that war criminals should die a million times. This sort of punishment can only happen in the

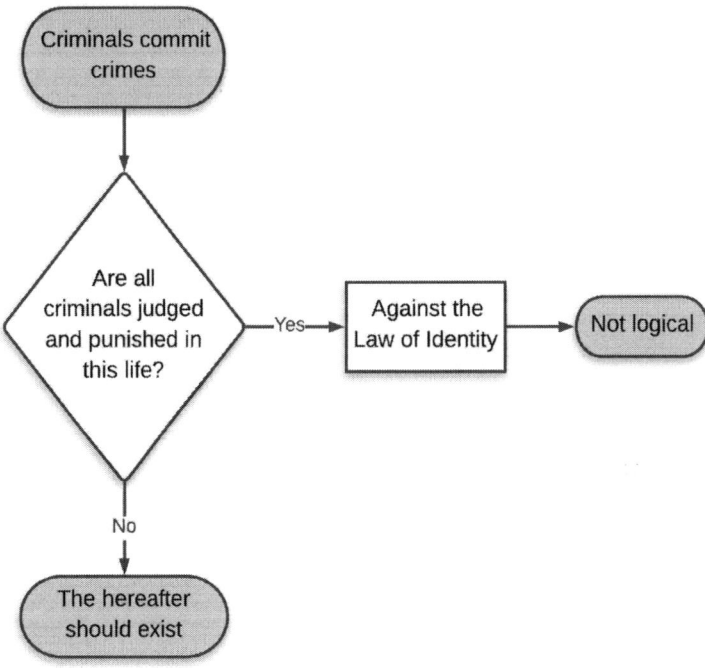

Logic flowchart 33: The proof of the hereafter – Example 2

hereafter as it is the place for final judgement and justice. If Allah SWT wants to punish a person a million times, He will do it.

[4:56] *(As for) those who disbelieve in Our communications, We shall make them enter fire; so oft as their skins are thoroughly burned, We will change them for other skins, that they may taste the chastisement; surely Allah is Mighty, Wise.*

As illustrated in logic flowchart 34, the statement saying that the maximum punishment of one penalty death for war criminals who killed millions of people is not fair or not equivalent to the crimes is a fact. Therefore, the opposite statement is against the Law of Identity and is not logical. Only in the hereafter would it be possible to punish war criminals by punishments that are equivalent to their crimes.

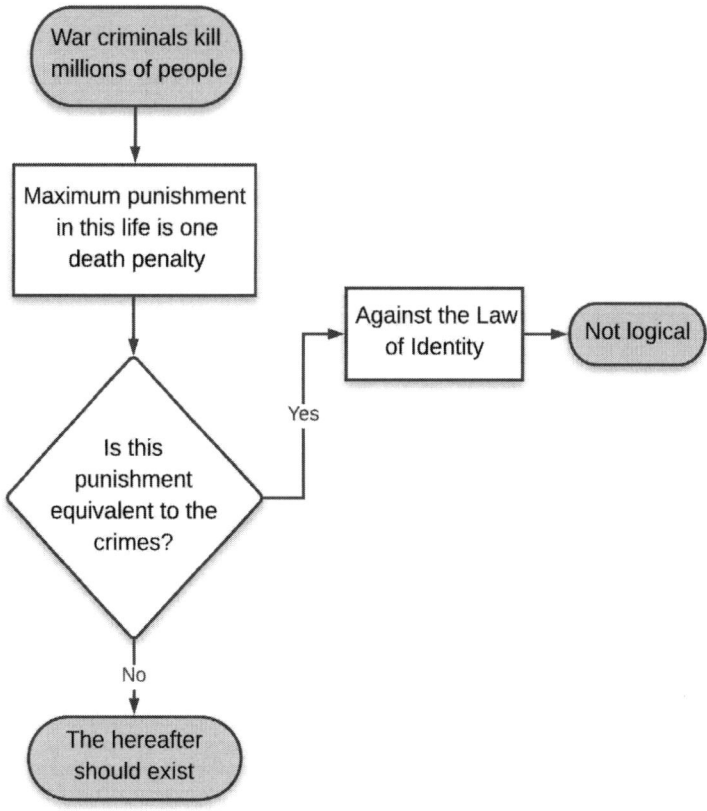

Logic flowchart 34: The proof of the hereafter – Example 3

Belief in the hereafter is an essential part of Islam belief, which has six pillars: belief in 1) Allah SWT, 2) His angels, 3) His messengers, 4) His books, 5) the hereafter and 6) the density. Therefore, if a Muslim does not believe in the hereafter, his belief is not complete.

Abu Huraira reported that one day the messenger of Allah PBUH appeared before the public when a man came up to him and said, "prophet of Allah, (tell me) what is Iman (faith)?" Upon this, he (the Holy prophet) replied, "That you affirm your faith in Allah, His angels, His Books, His meeting, His messengers and that you affirm your faith in the resurrection hereafter." (Sahih Muslim, Book #001, Hadith #0004)

As the hereafter should exist for the reasons mentioned above, what is the proof that paradise and hell exist? What are the reasons for creating paradise and hell in the hereafter? This is the topic in the next section.

4.2 Do paradise and hell exist?

The logic in the existence of paradise and hell is linked to the understanding that this life is like a test for humans. Allah SWT has created life and death to try, reward or punish people in the hereafter according to their deeds.

[67:2] *Who created death and life that He may try you; which of you is best in deeds; and He is the Mighty, the Forgiving.*

It is common sense that a human who does good does not have the same status as the one who does evil. For example, a student who spends a long time to prepare and study for his exam will be rewarded by passing his exam, while a student who does not study and wastes his time on useless things will not pass his exam, which is a sort of punishment for him. Similarly, paradise and hell are the reward and punishment for the test that humans undergo in this life.

A comparison between a student's exam and a human's test is illustrated in logic flowchart 35. The logic implies that the student who studies and answers his exam's questions correctly will be rewarded by passing his exam, whereas the student who does not study will be punished by failing his exam. Similarly, a human who searches for his creator and does efforts to recognise Allah SWT will be rewarded by going to paradise in the hereafter, whereas a human who does no efforts to recognise his creator, will be punished by going to hell.

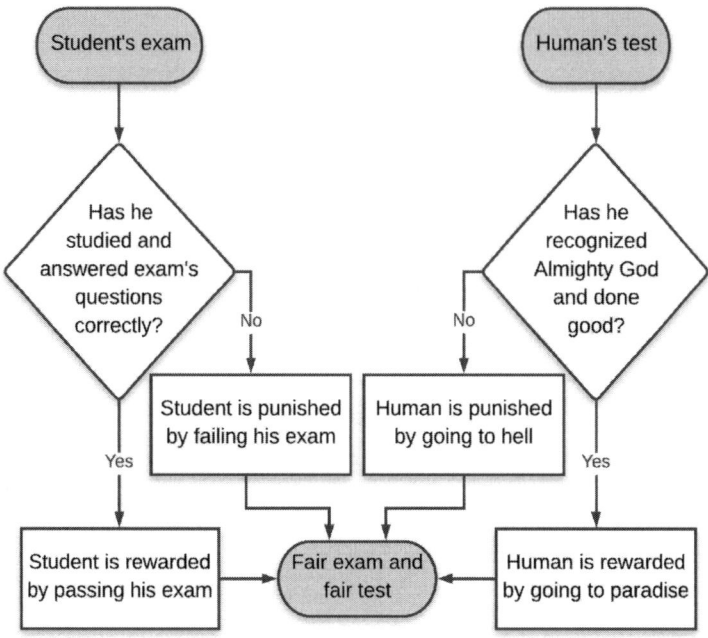

Logic flowchart 35: The paradise and hell – Example 1

In fact, as mentioned earlier, humans are the most important creatures of Almighty God, have been honoured by Almighty God and have been made greater than all other creatures. Therefore, we will be judged for our deeds by Allah SWT. But we have to remember that the mercy of Allah SWT is tremendously large. As mentioned by the prophet PBUH, Allah SWT has created hundreds of mercies, each one as large as the distance between the earth and heaven. Only one mercy was sent to the earth between human, animals and other creatures. The remaining 99 mercies are kept for the day of judgement for all humans.

Abu Huraira reported Allah's messenger PBUH as saying, "There are one hundred (parts of) mercy for Allah and He has sent down out of these one part of mercy upon the jinn and human beings and the insects and it is because of this (one part) that they love one another, show kindness to one another and even the beast treats its young one with affection, and Allah has reserved 99 parts of mercy with which He would treat His servants on the Day of resurrection." (Sahih Muslim, Book #037, Hadith #6631)

Furthermore, the prophet PBUH said Allah SWT has for His slaves more mercy than the mother for her child.

Narrated Umar bin Al-Khattab: Some Sabi (i.e. war prisoners, children and woman only) were brought before the prophet and behold, a woman amongst them was milking her breasts to feed and whenever she found a child amongst the captives, she took it over her chest and nursed it (she had lost her child but later she found him). The prophet said to us, "Do you think that this lady can throw her son in the fire?" We replied, "No, if she has the power not to throw it (in the fire)." The prophet then said, "Allah is more merciful to His slaves than this lady to her son." (Sahih Bukhari, Book #73, Hadith #28)

Allah SWT said in the holy Quran that His mercy encompasses all things:

[7:156] *He said, "(As for) My chastisement, I will afflict with it whom I please, and My mercy encompasses all things."*

The scholars have concluded that the paradise is forever, while hell is not forever and will be ended. This can be seen in the following verses from the holy Quran. When Allah SWT talks about paradise, He said 'forever'.

[98:7-8] *(As for) those who believe and do good, surely they are the best of men. Their reward with their Lord is gardens of perpetuity beneath which rivers flow, abiding therein forever.*

While in the same chapter when Allah SWT talks about the hell, He did not say 'forever'.

[98:6] *Surely those who disbelieve from amongst the followers of the Book and the polytheists shall be in the fire of hell, abiding therein; they are the worst of men.*

The scholars also said that paradise is much larger than hell. Allah mentioned in different verses in the holy Quran that paradise is as big as between the earth and heavens.

[3:133] *And hasten to forgiveness from your Lord; and a Garden, the extensiveness of which is (as) the heavens and the earth, it is prepared for the righteous.*

[57:21] *Hasten to forgiveness from your Lord and to a garden the extensiveness of which is as the extensiveness of the heaven and the earth; it is prepared for those who believe in Allah and His messengers.*

Hell was never intended to occupy a large space. It has been said that it has a very limited narrow space.

[25:13] *And when they are cast into a narrow place in it, bound, they shall there call out for destruction.*

Life in paradise will have completely different conditions from life on earth. In paradise, life is forever and the people do not get old. In other words, their bodies will always stay young, similar to that at the age of 33 years old in this worldly life. In fact, we can say that time does not exist in paradise. This means that the laws of nature as we know on earth, such as the gravity of Newton and the relativity of Einstein, are not applicable in paradise. However, there will be new laws that guarantee eternal life. Consequently, the people in paradise will have bodies that are completely different from our bodies in our present life. Their bodies will have the capability to live forever, not get old and never die, e.g. cells will not die. There will also be no dirt in paradise, so their bodies will not produce waste as we know in this life.

The people in paradise will not require food for their bodies to survive. Instead, food will be there to be enjoyed. Indeed, our prophet said that body waste of the people in paradise will not be excreted as in our present life. Rather, it will leave our body like sweat that has a very nice odour. In other words, paradise is a completely different environment that has its own laws and conditions.

Many verses in the holy Quran support the idea that life in paradise is different from, and not to be compared with life on earth. The following verses describe new and different creations in the hereafter.

[21:104] *On the day when We will roll up heaven like the rolling up of the scroll for writings, as We originated the first creation, (so) We shall reproduce it; a promise (binding on Us); surely We will bring it about.*

[14:48] *On the day when the earth shall be changed into a different earth, and the heavens (as well), and they shall come forth before Allah, the One, the Supreme.*

Fruit in paradise is different.

[2:25] *And convey good news to those who believe and do good deeds, that they shall have gardens in which rivers flow; whenever they shall be given a portion of the fruit thereof, they shall say: This is what was given to us before; and they shall be given the like of it.*

[56:32-33] *And abundant fruit, neither intercepted nor forbidden.*

Wine in paradise is different.

[56:18-19] *With goblets and ewers and a cup of pure drink; They shall not be affected with headache thereby, nor shall they get exhausted.*

The rivers in paradise are different.

[47:15] *A parable of the garden which those guarding (against evil) are promised: Therein are rivers of water that does not alter, and rivers of milk the taste whereof does not change, and rivers of drink delicious to those who drink, and rivers of honey clarified.*

People's feelings for each other are also different in paradise.

[15:47] *And We will root out whatever of rancor is in their hearts, (they shall be) as brethren, on raised couches, face to face.*

No one can comprehend exactly how paradise will be.

[32:17] *So no soul knows what is hidden for them of that which will refresh the eyes; a reward for what they did.*

Similarly, the fire in hell is different from the fire that we know in our life on earth. The fire in hell is not like a burning oven as we know in our life. People of hell talk to each other, as in our current life.

[7:38] *whenever a nation shall enter (the hell), it shall curse its sister, until when they have all come up with one another into it; the last of them shall say with regard to the foremost of them: Our Lord! these led us astray therefore give them a double chastisement of the fire.*

[43:77] *And they shall call out: O Malik! let your Lord make an end of us. He shall say: Surely you shall tarry.*

[33:66] *On the day when their faces shall be turned back into the fire, they shall say: O would that we had obeyed Allah and obeyed the messenger!*

There are trees in hell, but different from the trees on earth.

[37:64-66] *Surely it is a tree that-grows in the bottom of the hell; Its produce is as it were the heads of the serpents. Then most surely they shall eat of it and fill (their) bellies with it.*

There is also water in hell, but different from our water on earth.

[44:48] *Then pour above his head of the torment of the boiling water.*

[37:67] *Then most surely they shall have after it to drink of a mixture prepared in boiling water.*

The body of the people of hell will not be like our bodies in the present life and can change its skin.

[4:56] *(As for) those who disbelieve in Our communications, We shall make them enter fire; so oft as their skins are thoroughly burned, We will change them for other skins, that they may taste the chastisement; surely Allah is Mighty, Wise.*

The mercy of Almighty God for the people of hell is that their life will be whole and they will get used to it. This kind of evil soul, which deserves to be in hell, cannot live in peace. During their life on earth, they fight, start wars, and hate and harm people, so it is only just for them to stay in the fire. This kind of soul is an evil soul, did evil on earth and will always do evil.

[6:27-28] *And could you see when they are made to stand before the fire, then they shall say: Would that we were sent back, and we would not reject the communications of our Lord and we would be of the believers. Nay, what they concealed before shall become manifest to them; and if they were sent back, they would certainly go back to that which they are forbidden, and most surely they are liars.*

In fact, our present life compromises both paradise and hell. We practise paradise and hell in each moment in our daily life. On the one hand, good things happen to us; good feelings, moments of happiness, laughter, love and enjoyment of life are all part of paradise. On the other hand, bad things also happen to us; bad feelings, moments of sadness, illness, death and suffering in life are all part of hell. Therefore, if both paradise and hell exist partially in our present life, they should also exist in the hereafter. However, in the hereafter, paradise and hell will be separated and completely independent of one another. If Allah SWT created this life as partially paradise and partially hell, He can create them independently in the hereafter.

As illustrated in logic flowchart 36, our present life compromises two parts, namely partial paradise and partial hell. Partial means that it exists only in part or is incomplete. As we have logically proven in chapter 2, this life has been created, so the statement saying that Almighty God created partial paradise and partial hell is correct. Therefore, the statement saying that Almighty God cannot create paradise and hell independently is against the Law of Non-Contradiction.

As demonstrated above, paradise and hell should exist. But who will go to paradise and who will go to hell? Will only Muslims go to paradise and non-Muslims to hell? How will Allah SWT evaluate different people? These questions will be answered in the next section.

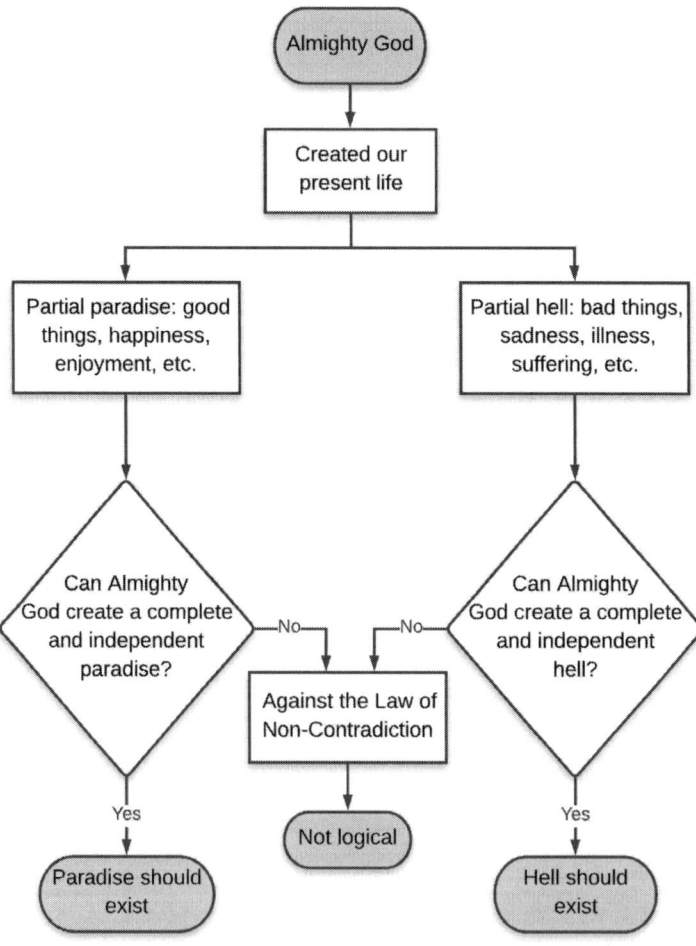

Logic flowchart 36: The paradise and hell – Example 2

4.3   Will non-Muslims go to paradise or hell?

Firstly, the judgement over any human being, whether he will go to paradise or to hell, is only in the hands of Allah SWT. Only Allah SWT decides over His creatures and judges them. Allah SWT will question every human about his deeds and no one can question Him.

[21:23] *He cannot be questioned concerning what He does and they shall be questioned.*

Therefore, every human being will be judged by Almighty God and asked about his deeds in this worldly life. However, a person, in any place in the world, is different from others and his circumstances are unique. Everyone has grown up in a specific environment, in a specific culture and has parents with a certain religion, level of education and background. All these factors have not been chosen by the person himself, but they affect his behaviour, belief and level of intellect. As Allah SWT is the most just and He will never do wrong to His creatures, His judgement of any person will be based on all the unique factors associated with that person.

Everyone is unique, and therefore two persons having the same experiences in their lives do not exist. Thus, everyone will be judged according to their unique circumstances. For example, someone who was born in a Muslim country from Muslim parents, and who lived in an Islamic environment and a Muslim culture is in fact from the nation of Islam and the nation of Mohammed PBUH. Another person, who was born in a non-Muslim country from non-Muslim parents, and who lived in a non-Islamic environment and non-Muslim culture has a completely different situation and will be judged differently. This concept is illustrated in logic flowchart 37. As different people are born in different circumstances, it is logic and just that they will have different tests and different judgements.

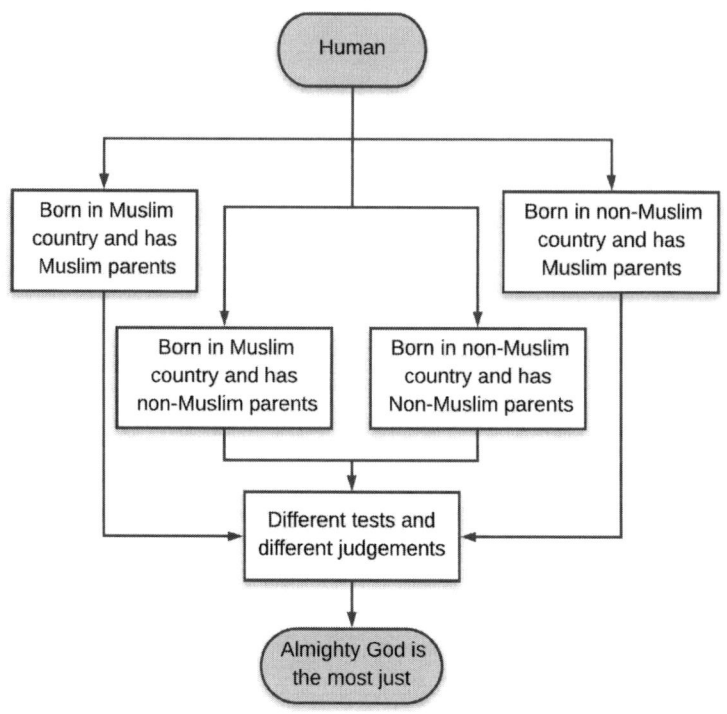

Logic flowchart 37: Non-Muslims – Example 1

Everyone has a completely different test and in turn, the model answer to his test will be different. In other words, some specific deeds might be expected from a certain person to pass his test, but not expected from another person. The level of expectations depends on the kind of test. For example, it is not possible to evaluate an exam of an engineering student based on model answers of a non-engineering course. Allah SWT is the best example and is the most just.

A comparison between a student's exam and a human's test is illustrated in logic flowchart 38. The statement saying that a student who studies engineering will not be evaluated using model answers of a non-engineering course is a fact. Similarly, the statement saying that a human who is born Muslim will be evaluated using model answers of a human who is born non-Muslim is a fact. Therefore, the opposite statements are against the Law of Identity.

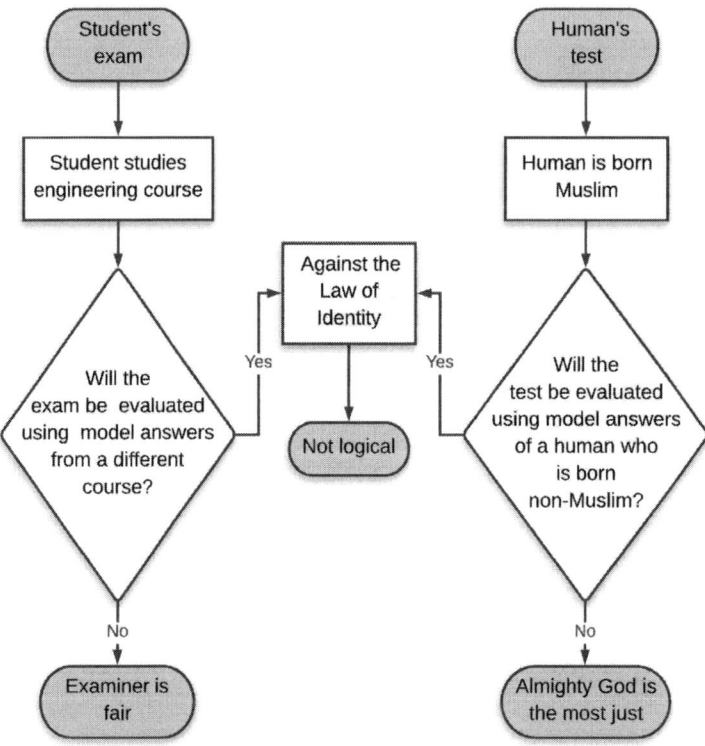

Logic flowchart 38: Non-Muslims – Example 2

Muslim scholars indicated that there are three types of non-Muslim people:
1. Those who did not hear about the message of Islam. This type will not be punished.
2. Those who heard wrong or confusing information about the message of Islam. This second type is the same as the first type, i.e. they will not be punished.

3. Those who heard clearly and correctly about the message of Islam and intentionally rejected it. This third type is the one that will be punished.

Obviously only Almighty God can know about every single person and classify him in one of the three types. As illustrated in logic flowchart 39, the justice of Almighty God implies that only people who heard correctly about the message of the Islam and intentionally rejected it will be punished.

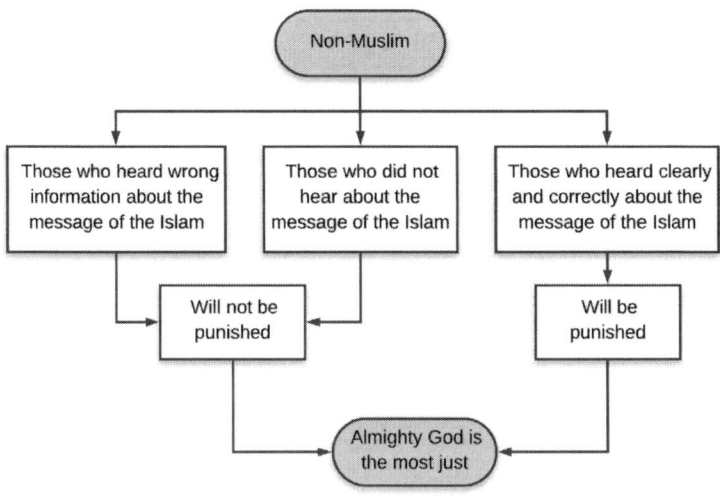

Logic flowchart 39: Non-Muslims – Example 3

In fact, throughout history, every nation has had a warner or a messenger, as Allah SWT said in the holy Quran.

[35:24] *Surely We have sent you with the truth as a bearer of good news and a warner; and there is not a people but a warner has gone amongst them.*

[16:36] *And certainly We raised in every nation a messenger saying: Serve Allah and shun the Shaitan.*

Allah SWT has not mentioned all messengers in the holy Quran or other holy scriptures, but there were thousands of messengers and we do not have any information about them.

[40:78] *And certainly We sent messengers before you: there are some of them that We have mentioned to you and there are others whom We have not mentioned to you.*

If we go back in history, we will find that most nations that believe in one god have had a messenger.

[2:62] *Surely those who believe, and those who are Jews, and the Christians, and the Sabians, whoever believes in Allah and the Last day and does good, they shall have their reward from their Lord, and there is no fear for them, nor shall they grieve.*

The Sabians are those who worshipped the sun with the intention to get closer to Almighty God because it is a sign from Him. Even if they did not receive the message of the Islam correctly, the Sabians will get their reward from Almighty God. In fact, most religions were originally one, but throughout history, people have changed them. This topic will be dealt with in chapter 7, the Islam (the last religion).

The mercy of Allah SWT is great and varies from person to person and from situation to situation. People who lived at the time of prophets have seen the miracles with their own eyes, while other people did not. The people who lived at the time of Moses PBUH have seen him opening the sea with a stick, and the people who lived at the time of Jesus PBUH have seen him raising the dead. However, we who live now have not seen that: we have just heard about it and seeing is different from hearing.

Therefore, the mercy of Allah SWT varies as one sees the miracles but the other just heard. These are in fact different levels of the test. The people who lived at the time of prophets had an easy test as they have seen the miracles. However, the people living now, long after the time of prophets, have a difficult test.

Actually, the ones who saw the miracles did not necessarily become believers, which may not be a mercy for the nonbelievers who lived in the time of prophets and did not obey them. For example, the people of Jesus PBUH asked for a miracle and when they saw it, they still did not believe.

[5:112] *When the disciples said: O Isa son of Marium! will your Lord consent to send down to us food from heaven? He said: Be careful of (your duty to) Allah if you are believers.*

[5:115] *Allah said: Surely I will send it down to you, but whoever shall disbelieve afterwards from amongst you, surely I will chastise him with a chastisement with which I will not chastise, anyone amongst the nations.*

Generally, when miracles are sent (easy test), the punishment of Almighty God will be very severe for nonbelievers (difficult judgement). Therefore, the judgement of the people who saw the miracles is much more severe than the judgement of those who just heard of them. This is a logical way of judgement as Allah SWT is the most just.

As illustrated in flowchart 40, the justice of Allah SWT implies that the level of judgement will be according to the level of test, i.e. easy, average or difficult.

The holy Quran in the hand of the Muslim nation is a proof that they have received the message fully, correctly and clearly from the prophet PBUH. Muslims who were born with the holy Quran in their hands, in their parents' home and in their countries, will have a more difficult judgement than other people who were born and who grew up in different situations. Therefore, the holy Quran can be either a mercy for Muslims who follow its instructions or an argument against them if they do not follow. It is mentioned in the holy Quran that Almighty God will not torture people without sending a messenger.

[17:15] *Whoever goes aright, for his own soul does he go aright; and whoever goes astray, to its detriment only does he go astray:*

nor can the bearer of a burden bear the burden of another, nor do We chastise until We raise a messenger.

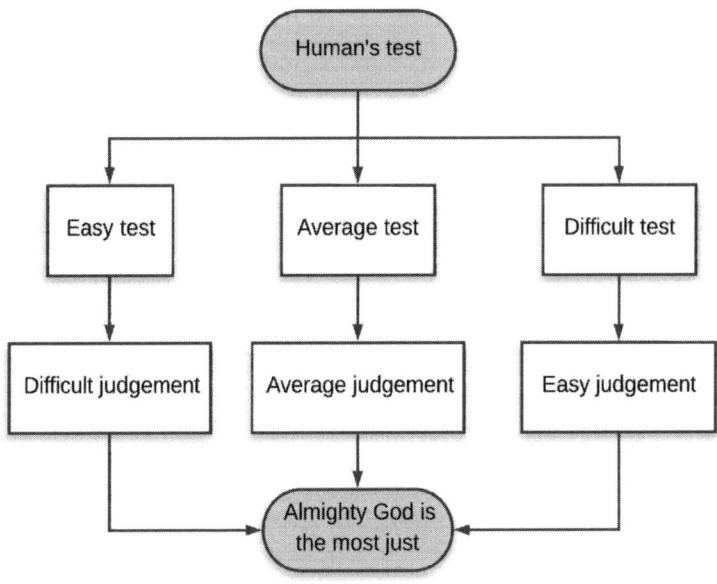

Logic flowchart 40: Non-Muslims – Example 4

To summarise the conclusion of this section, we combine flowchart 37 with flowchart 40 to demonstrate the justice of Allah SWT in evaluating humans. As shown in logic flowchart 41, the evaluation of human tests can be classified into four categories:
1. People who were born in a Muslim country and have Muslim parents have an easy test and difficult judgement.
2. People who were born in a non-Muslim country and have Muslim parents have an average test and average judgement.
3. People who were born in a Muslim country and have non-Muslim parents have an average test and average judgement.
4. People who were born in a non-Muslim country and have non-Muslim parents have a difficult test and easy judgement.

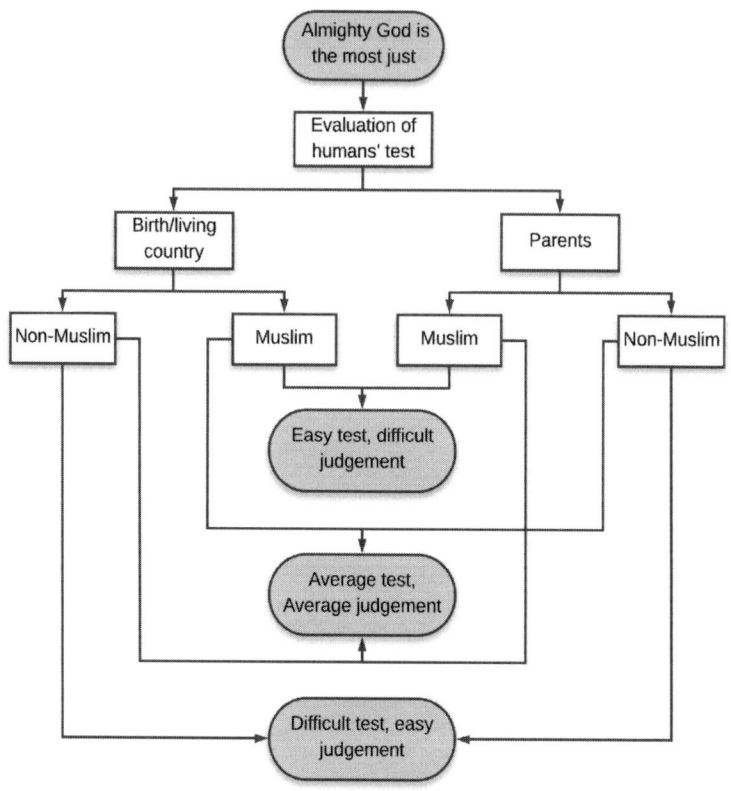

Logic flowchart 41: Non-Muslims – Example 5

5 Destiny and freedom of choice

5.1 Do we choose our deeds or are they written for us?

There are many things that we do not choose in our life, for example, our skin colour, nationality and country of birth, our height, shape, eye colour, etc. These are not, and should not, be our choice because they are only under the control of Almighty God.

[28:68] *And your Lord creates and chooses whom He pleases; to choose is not theirs; glory be to Allah, and exalted be He above what they associate (with Him).*

However, there are many other things that we can choose, such as our test from Allah SWT to recognise and worship Him. We can choose to do good deeds or to do bad deeds, to be honest or to be dishonest, to tell the truth or to lie, etc. We can choose to search, recognise, and worship Almighty God. We can choose to follow the messengers sent by Allah SWT. These are the things we are free to choose and on which we will be judged. Therefore, Almighty God will not judge us on things that we cannot choose, but He will ask us only about the things within our free choice.

It is logical and obvious that a human chooses many different things in various life situations. He can choose to study engineering, medicine, music or law. He can choose to participate in the kind of sport he likes, e.g. football, judo, karate or swimming. Indeed, the function of our brain is to choose between the different possibilities that we see in different situations during our life.

As illustrated in logic flowchart 42, human life consists of two parts. The first part compromises the things that we do not choose and will not be judged, while the second part comprises the things that we choose and will be judged. This demonstrates the justice of Almighty God, who is the most just.

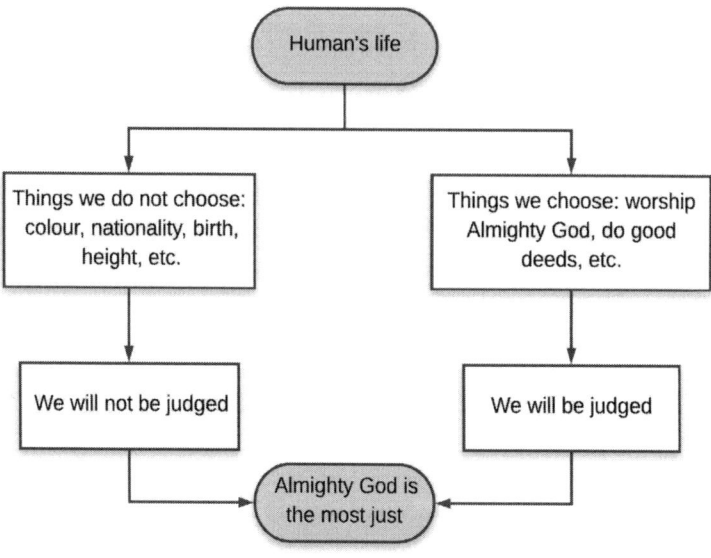

Logic flowchart 42: The destiny – Example 1

If someone attacks you in the street, you would not say that Almighty God wrote this for you and you do not take any action. The logical decision is to defend yourself, take action against the attacker and report the incident to the authorities. Therefore, in this case you have a choice, but Allah SWT with His infinite knowledge knows what will happen and what action you will take.

The knowledge of Allah SWT is unlimited, as He knows everything about past, present and future. In fact, for Almighty God, there is no present, past or future as He is above time. He created time, therefore, He knows the future exactly in the same way as He knows the past and the present. Therefore, if we say that Allah SWT knows what you will do, it does not mean that you do not have a choice to do what you want.

As demonstrated earlier in this chapter, for a part of this life, we have no choice, but for another part we have free choice, as this life is the place for a test. In the hereafter, we have absolutely no choice, as the hereafter is the place for judgement, reward and punishment. A comparison between this life and next life is shown in logic flowchart 43.

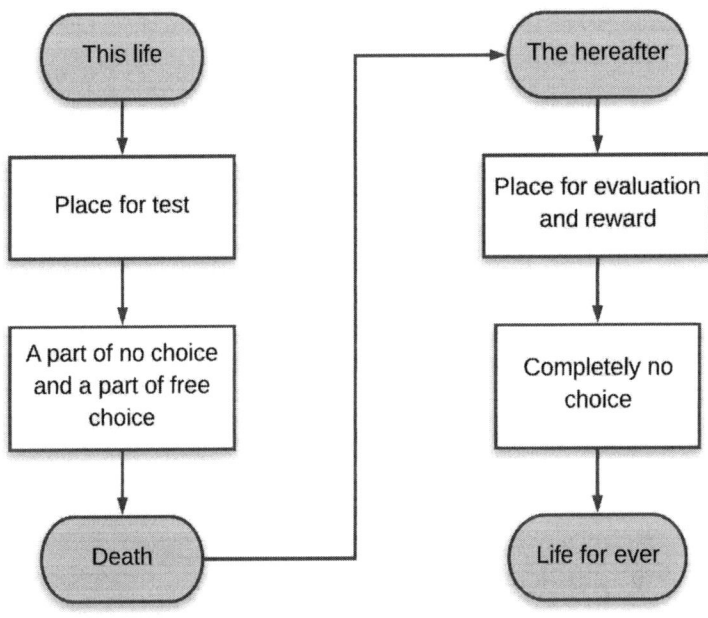

Logic flowchart 43: The destiny – Example 2

The freedom that Allah SWT gives to us is in fact His decision. In other words, Allah SWT has decided to give us the freedom to choose between good and evil.

[76:30] *But ye will not, except as Allah wills; for Allah is full of Knowledge and Wisdom.*

Allah SWT gives people the choice to believe:

[2:256] *There is no compulsion in religion; truly the right way has become clearly distinct from error.*

And He did not want to force them to believe:

[10:99] *And if your Lord wills, surely all those who are in the earth would have believed, all of them; will you then force men till they become believers?*

If, on the first day of the school year, a teacher provided the students with a list of names of those who will pass the course and those who will fail, none of the student would study or do any effort during the school year. Similarly, if a human thought that his deeds were written for him, his destiny to paradise or hell was already known and he had no choice, he would not be motivated to do anything in his life.

It is not logical to assume that a teacher would decide that certain students will pass their exam before the start of the school year, and that he would then evaluate them at the end of the year. Similarly, it is not logical to assume that Allah SWT has decided good or bad deeds for us in this worldly life before He created us, and that He would evaluate us in the hereafter.

This concept is illustrated in logic flowchart 44. The statement saying that the teacher will not decide on who will pass or fail his course before the start of the school year is a fact. Similarly, the statement saying that Allah will not decide who will go to paradise or to hell before the start of creation is a fact. Therefore, the opposite statements are against the Law of Identity and are not logical.

Muslim scholars say that those who think that they have no choice in this life are telling lies and do not believe in Allah SWT. This conclusion is based on the following verse from the holy Quran.

[6:148] *Those who are polytheists will say: If Allah had pleased we would not have associated (aught with Him) nor our fathers, nor would we have forbidden (to ourselves) anything; even so did those before them reject until they tasted Our punishment. Say: Have you any knowledge with you so you should bring it forth to us? You only follow a conjecture and you only tell lies.*

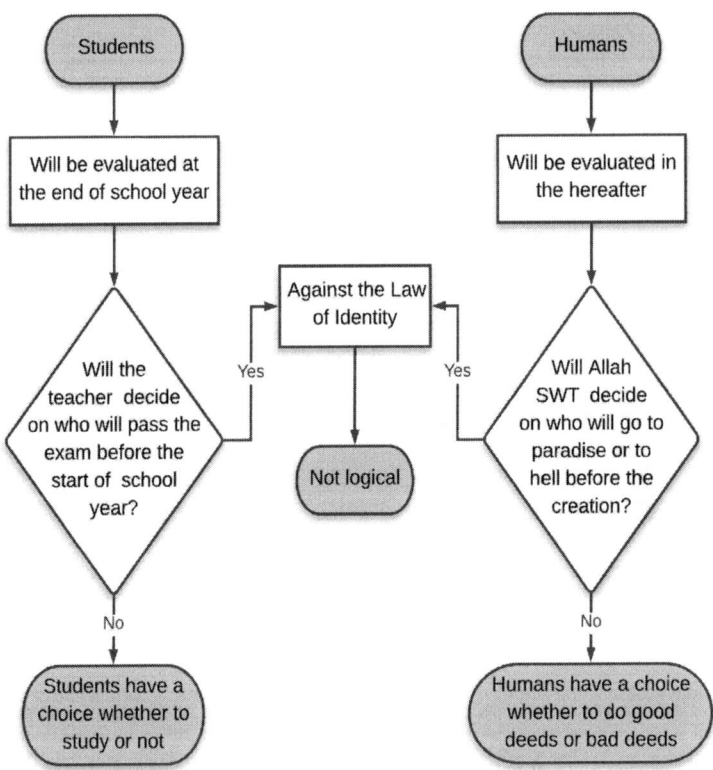

Logic flowchart 44: The destiny - Example 3

If Allah SWT forced us to worship Him, there should be no reward. Similarly, if Allah SWT forced us not to believe in Him, there should be no punishment. Therefore, Allah SWT gives us the freedom to choose whether to worship Him or not so that we would deserve either reward or punishment in the hereafter.

There are many verses in the holy Quran indicating that humans are free to choose between good and evil.

[3:145] *And whoever desires the reward of this world, I shall give him of it, and whoever desires the reward of the hereafter I shall give him of it, and I will reward the grateful.*

[76:29] *Surely this is a reminder, so whoever pleases takes to his Lord a way.*

[91:7-8] *And the soul and Him Who made it perfect. Then He inspired it to understand what is right and wrong for it.*

Because humans possess an intellect, they are the highest level of creatures on earth. All other living creatures, such as plants and animals, do not possess such intellect. Plants, animals and humans have the characteristic to grow, while only animals and humans have the characteristics to move, eat, feel emotions and have physical interaction. However, only humans have the characteristic of rational and logical thinking. In other words, they possess an intellect. Therefore, human nature can be divided into three parts: a) growing up like plants, b) moving like animals and

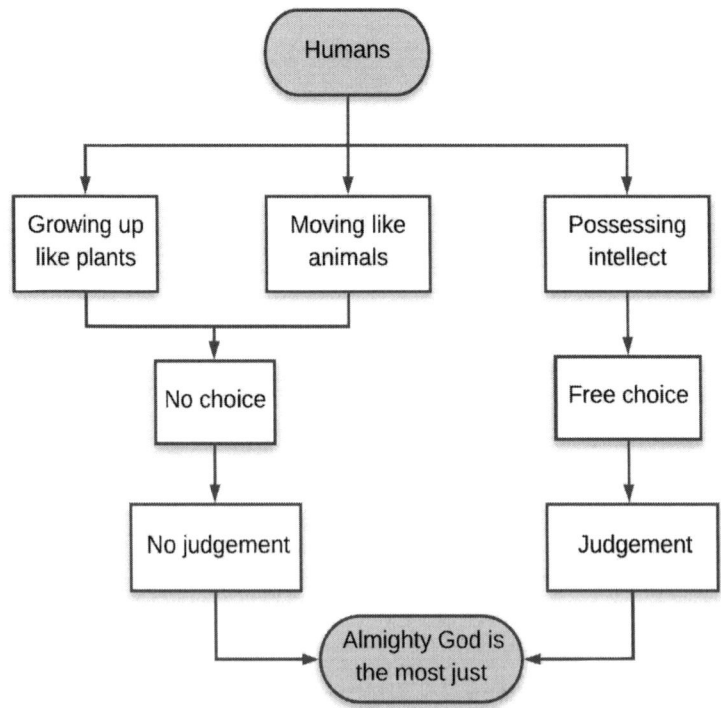

Logic flowchart 45: The destiny - Example 4

c) thinking by using the mind. The first two parts do not allow humans to choose. We are born, grow up, eat, drink, have spiritual emotions and move physically, but we do not have any control over or an option to choose or change these things. However, the third part, our intellect, allows us to choose, which distinguishes us from plants and animals. As Allah SWT is the most just, we will only be judged on the third part – the use of our intellect – as illustrated in logic flowchart 45.

6 The holy Quran

6.1 Has prophet Mohammed PBUH copied the holy Quran from the Bible and the Torah?

As Muslims, we believe in all holy books revealed by Almighty God, including the holy Quran, the original Bible and the original Torah (first testament). The similarity between all three books reveals that all of them are from the same one god, Allah SWT.

All three books have the same values and morality, and motivate people to worship only one god. Each book has revealed the correction of changes and corruption made by people in previous books. The Bible has revealed the correction of changes made by the Jews in the first testament regarding the description of Almighty God and His messengers.

[3:50] *And (I come) confirming that which was before me of the Torah, and to make lawful some of that which was forbidden unto you. I come unto you with a sign from your Lord, so keep your duty to Allah and obey me.*

The holy Quran was revealed to correct the changes made in the Bible, especially the concept of father and son, which wrongly associates a partner with Allah SWT. The holy Quran returns to the original message from Almighty God 'there is only one god, worship only one god and do not associate any partner with Almighty God, who is complete and perfect'. This message is the original one that has been revealed to all messengers sent by Allah SWT and was stated in the original Bible and Torah.

The holy Quran clearly says to Christian people 'you are wrong. Your concept of father and son is not correct as it associates a partner with Almighty God'. Similarly, at the time of the prophet Mohammed PBUH, the Jews associated a partner with Allah SWT by saying that one of their prophets is the son of god. The holy Quran corrects this wrong concept.

[9:30] *And the Jews say: Uzair is the son of Allah; and the Christians say: The Messiah is the son of Allah; these are the words of their mouths; they imitate the saying of those who disbelieved before; may Allah destroy them; how they are turned away!*

Therefore, it is not logical to assume that the prophet Mohammed PBUH has copied the holy Quran from the Bible and the Torah. How can this be if he is telling the Jews and Christians that their concepts are wrong and flawed, and they have to go back to the original concept and the original message of Almighty God? If the prophet Mohammed PBUH had copied the holy Quran from previous holy books, he would have copied everything, including the mistakes and corrupted concepts introduced by humans.

Furthermore, some contradictions between the holy Quran on the one side, and the Bible and Torah on the other side, confirm that it is not possible to assume that the holy Quran was copied from them. The Bible and Torah contradict modern science findings because people changed the original text of the Bible and Torah revealed by Almighty God. However, the holy Quran does not contradict modern science findings. For example, the Bible mentions that the earth and heaven were created in six days and indicates that a day is 24 hours. However, the holy Quran mentions only six days and does not indicate that a day is 24 hours. In Arabic, a day may mean a weekday or a period of time. Even in English, a day may mean a particular period of the past or an era. Therefore, the Bible contradicts modern science, but the holy Quran does not.

Another example is that the Bible mentions that day and night were created on the first day, while the stars and the sun were created on the fourth day. This clearly contradicts modern science as it is not possible to have day and night before the creation of the sun. Furthermore, the Bible mentions that the earth was created on the third day, i.e. before the creation of the sun. This is again non-scientific and against modern science. If the prophet Mohammed PBUH had copied from the Bible, why did he not copy these false, humanly corrupted concepts?

Furthermore, the Bible mentions that Almighty God created two sources of light – the sun and moon – indicating that the moon has its own light. However, the holy Quran mentions that the sun is the source of light (a lamp) and the light of the moon is a reflected light.

[25:61] *Blessed is He Who made the constellations in the heavens and made therein a lamp and a shining moon.*

The above evidence indicates that it is not logical to assume that the holy Quran is copied from the Bible or Torah. The holy Quran does not contain the scientific mistakes found in the corrupted Bible and first testament. The holy Quran corrects the wrong concepts introduced by humans in the previous holy books.

A comparison between some concepts in the Bible and Torah on the one side and in the holy Quran on the other side is illustrated in logic flowchart 46. The statement saying that there are concepts in the Bible and Torah which contradict modern science is a fact. Furthermore, the statement saying that the concepts in the holy Quran do not contradict modern science is also a fact. Therefore, the statement saying that the holy Quran corrects the concepts in the Bible and Torah is a fact and implies that the holy Quran cannot be copied from the Bible and Torah. Therefore, the opposite statement saying that the holy Quran does not correct concepts in the Bible and Torah is against the Law of Identity and is not logical.

Further evidence that the holy Quran is not copied from the Bible and Torah is that the holy Quran was written in Arabic, while the other two scriptures were written in a foreign, non-Arabic language.

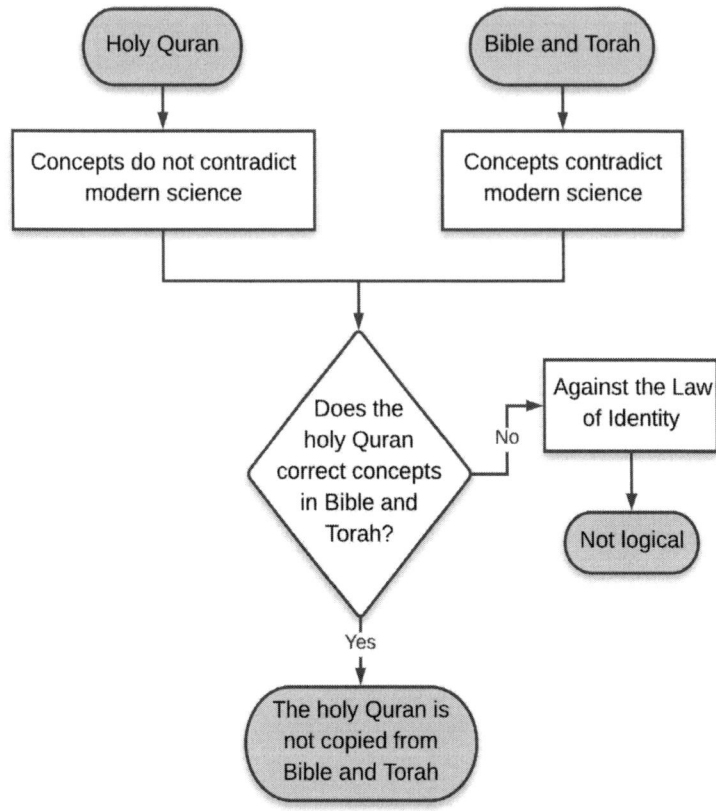

Logic flowchart 46: The holy Quran - Example 1

[16:103] *We know indeed that they say, "It is a man that teaches him." The tongue of him they wickedly point to is notably foreign, while this is Arabic, pure and clear.*

The first translation of the Bible into Arabic was done 1,000 years after the revelation of the holy Quran. Furthermore, contact between the prophet PBUH and the Jews and Christians happened only after he moved to Medina, i.e. 13 years after the beginning of the revelation. The prophet gave them the information revealed to him by Almighty God and many of them accepted Islam, so it could not be the other way around, i.e. the Jews and Christians followed the message of prophet Mohammed PBUH.

The similarities between the holy Quran, Bible and first testament indicate that all three books are from the same origin, Allah SWT. For example, a student uses a certain book as a reference for his assignment, and another student uses the same book for a similar assignment. This does not mean that the two students are copying each other's work; only the source they are using is the same. Similarly, we can say that the holy Quran, Bible and Torah did not copy each other, but they are from the same source – Allah SWT.

[3:3] *He has revealed to you the Book with truth, verifying that which is before it, and He revealed the Torah and the Gospel.*

[7:157] *Those who follow the messenger, the Prophet who can neither read nor write, whom they will find described in the Torah and the Gospel (which are) with them. He will enjoin on them that which is right and forbid them that which is wrong. He will make lawful for them all good things and prohibit for them only the foul; and he will relieve them of their burden and the fetters that they used to wear. Then those who believe in him, and honour him, and help him, and follow the light which is sent down with him: they are the successful.*

As illustrated in logic flowchart 47, a teacher produces lecture notes for his course and asks students to write a report. The statement saying that the reports of student A and student B should contain similar information is a fact. Similarly, Allah SWT revealed His holy scriptures to several prophets. Therefore, the statement saying that the holy Quran should contain similar information to the Bible and Torah is a fact. Therefore, the opposite statement is against the Law of Identity and is not logical.

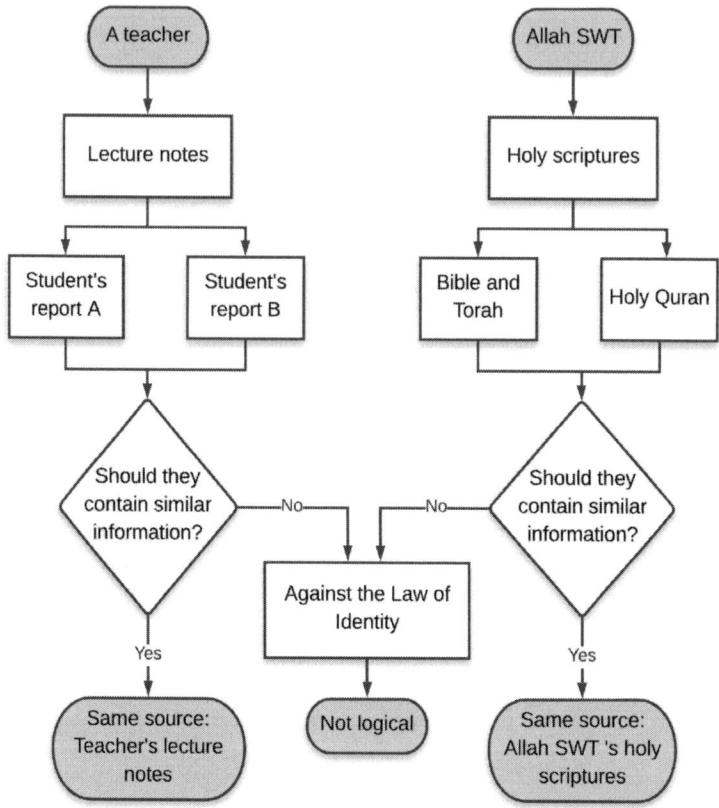

Logic flowchart 47: The holy Quran - Example 2

As the holy Quran is not copied from the Bible or Torah, what is special in the holy Quran? What is the miracle in the holy Quran? Who can clearly see and comprehend this miracle? This is the next topic in this chapter.

6.2 What is the miracle of the holy Quran?

Every prophet has miracles from Allah SWT to show to his people so that they would believe in his message. These miracles have been witnessed by people at that time. For example, some of the miracles of Moses PBUH were, for example: the stick turning into a serpent, his hand becoming bright white, the flood, the lice, the frogs and the blood. The miracles of Jesus PBUH were, for example: healing the blind and the leper, the resurrection of the dead, the provisions of today and tomorrow, i.e. telling people what they have in their houses, and a table laden with food descending from heaven. Because the prophet Mohammed PBUH was the last prophet, his main miracle was not only witnessed by the people at that time, but it also remained a miracle forever. This miracle is the holy Quran.

The miracle of the holy Quran, which proves that the holy Quran is from Almighty God, is in its Arabic language. Arabic-speaking natives understand very well that the holy Quran is a miracle and could not have been written by a human. Allah SWT challenges all humans to bring a book like the holy Quran.

[17:88] *Say: If men and jinn should combine together to bring the like of this Quran, they could not bring the like of it, though some of them were aiders of others.*

A further challenge is to provide a single chapter similar to one in the holy Quran.

[10:38] *Or do they say: He (Mohammed) has forged it? Say: Then bring a chapter like this and invite whom you can besides Allah, if you are truthful.*

[2:23] *And if you are in doubt as to that which We have revealed to Our servant, then produce a chapter like it and call on your witnesses besides Allah if you are truthful.*

[2:24] *But if you do (it) not and never shall you do (it), then be on your guard against the fire of which men and stones are the fuel; it is prepared for the unbelievers.*

Until today, this challenge remains and will continue until the day of judgement. It is not only about providing some words and putting them together; it is about the rhetorical, literary and scientific miracles in the holy Quran. The style of the holy Quran and its content of knowledge, secrets and perfect Arabic language are beyond the style and knowledge of human beings. If we add to this that the prophet Mohammed PBUH was illiterate, it becomes impossible to assume that he wrote the holy Quran.

This challenge is the most amazing in history. Throughout history and until now, no human could rise up to such a challenge. No author ever wrote a book and challenged all people to write a similar one. The holy Quran challenged all humans to write a similar book, but nobody succeeded. Throughout history, many people have tried to write a similar text, but all of them failed. The logical conclusion is that the holy Quran is not written by a human, but that it is a revelation from Almighty God.

A Quran verse in itself is a miracle. There was no similar one before it was revealed and nobody could produce a similar one after it was revealed. It is not comparable to poetry, in which rhythm is based on the pronunciation of words. The rhythm of the holy Quran is not only based on the pronunciation of the words, but also on the meaning of the words. For example, the verses that talk about believers or paradise sound completely different than those that talk about nonbelievers and hell.

The concept of the miracle of the holy Quran in challenging humans to write a similar book is illustrated in logic flowchart 48. The statement saying that no human can write a similar book is a fact as no author could do it in the last 1,400 years. Therefore, the statement saying that a book similar to the holy Quran can be written by humans is against the Law of Identity.

Allah SWT clearly states that if the holy Quran is not His, it would contain a lot of contradictions.

[4:82] *Do they not then meditate on the Quran? And if it were from any other than Allah, they would have found in it many a discrepancy.*

No one can find any contradiction in the holy Quran. All the arguments of the nonbelievers who are trying to find

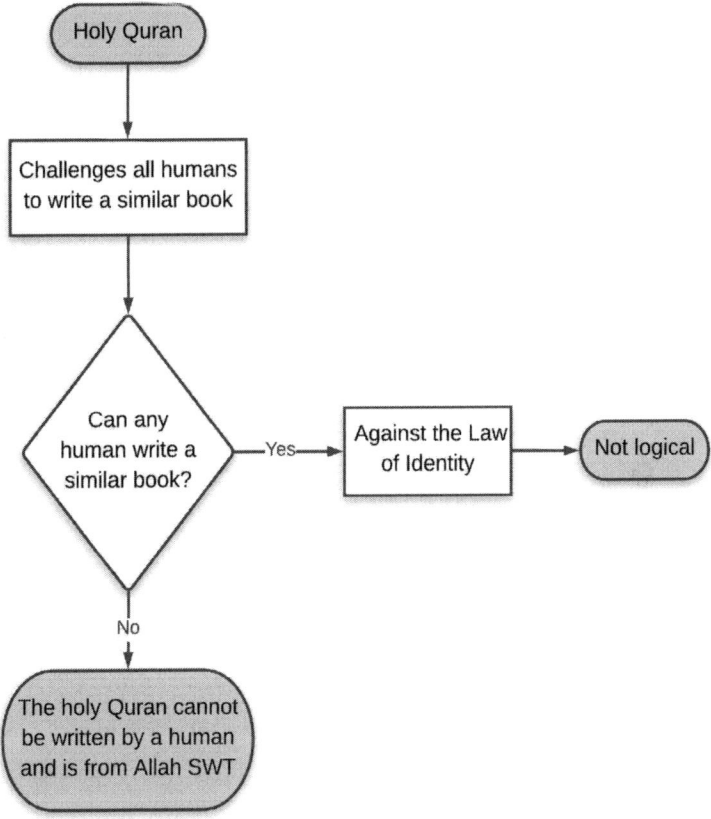

Logic flowchart 48: The holy Quran - Example 3

contradictions in the holy Quran, for instance on the internet, are mistranslations, misunderstandings, misinterpretations, out of context or not logical.

As the holy Quran is a miracle, what is the proof that Mohammed PBUH is not the author of the holy Quran? The next topic in this chapter answers the questions related to the proof that the holy Quran is not written by the prophet Mohammed PBUH himself.

6.3 Has prophet Mohammed PBUH written the holy Quran?

If the holy Quran was written by the prophet, we would see verses related to his problems, troubles and sadness during his life. But we do not see that in the holy Quran. His wife and his uncle, who strongly supported his message, died in one year, and we do not read anything about them in the holy Quran. His son, Ibrahim, died in his childhood, and yet we do not read anything about his death in the holy Quran. The holy Quran is completely separated from the life of the prophet PBUH. In contrast, in many situations, verses were revealed to criticise and correct the actions of the prophet PBUH.

For example, a blind man came to speak to the prophet Mohammed PBUH, but the prophet PBUH did not pay attention to him because he was busy with other people. The holy Quran blamed the prophet PBUH for his action against the blind man.

[80:1-4] *He frowned and turned (his) back, because there came to him the blind man. And what would make you know that he would purify himself, or become reminded so that the reminder should profit him?*

Furthermore, some verses criticise the actions of the prophet Mohammed PBUH.

[8:67] *It is not fit for a prophet that he should take captives unless he has fought and triumphed in the land; you desire the frail goods of this world, while Allah desires (for you) the hereafter; and Allah is Mighty, Wise.*

The holy Quran commands the prophet PBUH to tell his people that he does not know what will happen to them:

[46:9] *Say: I am not the first of the messengers, and I do not know what will be done with me or with you: I do not follow anything but that which is revealed to me, and I am nothing but a plain Warner.*

When Jews came to the prophet Mohammed PBUH and asked him about the soul, the people of the cave and a powerful king. The prophet PBUH told them "I will give you the answer tomorrow." He thought that the revelation would come to him by the next day. However, the revelation did not come with the answers the next day; it came after 15 days. During these 15 days, the prophet PBUH was very sad. The nonbelievers of Mecca were happy and some of the new Muslims doubted the message of Islam. As a result, Allah SWT criticised the prophet PBUH for promising to answer the questions without saying Insha'Allah (if Allah SWT wills).

[18:23-24] *And do not say of anything: Surely I will do it tomorrow. Unless Allah pleases; and remember your Lord when you forget and say: Maybe my Lord will guide me to a nearer course to the right than this.*

If the holy Quran was written by the prophet Mohammed PBUH, he would answer the questions the next day as he promised the Jews. This indecency proves that the holy Quran is a revelation from Almighty God and could not have been written by the prophet Mohammed PBUH.

The concepts presented above are summarised in logic flowchart 49. The statement saying that the holy Quran does not tell about the private life of the prophet Mohammed PBUH is a fact. Similarly, the statement saying that the holy Quran criticises and corrects the actions of the prophet Mohammed PBUH is also a fact. Therefore, the opposite statements are against the Law of Identity and not logical. Thus, the holy Quran cannot be written by the prophet Mohammed PBUH and should be the words of Allah SWT.

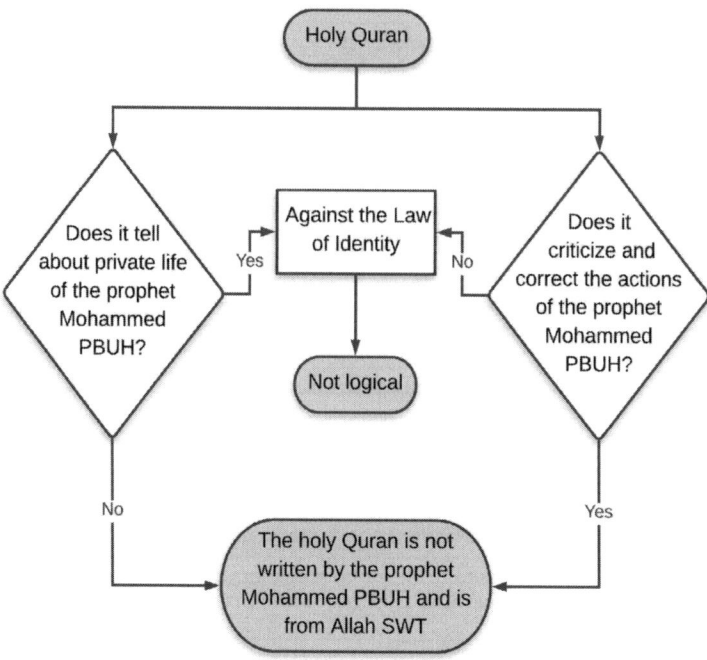

Logic flowchart 49: The holy Quran - Example 4

The holy Quran mentions that the best woman in the world and in all nations is Marium (Mary, the mother of Jesus PBUH).

[3:42] *And when the angels said: O Marium! surely Allah has chosen you and purified you and chosen you above the women of the world (of all nations).*

If this was not a revelation and was written by the prophet PBUH, it would mention that his mother, daughter or wife are the best women in the world. Why would the prophet PBUH mention Marium instead of a woman from his family?

It is well known in history that the prophet Mohammed PBUH did not want wealth. After his prophethood, there was no cooking in his house for a month or two. His wives protested and asked for a better life. However, the holy Quran criticised their protest.

[33:28] *O Prophet! say to your wives: If you desire this world's life and its adornment, then come, I will give you a provision and allow you to depart a goodly departing.*

[33:29] *And if you desire Allah and His messenger and the latter abode, then surely Allah has prepared for the doers of good amongst you a mighty reward.*

The wife of the prophet Aisha, may Allah SWT be pleased with her, said that months passed at their home without cooking. And when she was asked what they ate, she said, "Water and dates and our neighbours gave us milk." Therefore, the prophet lived this poor life at the time that he was the leader of the Islamic empire and he could live like a king. When he passed away, he did not leave any wealth or money for his family.

When his son Ibrahim died, a solar eclipse took place the same day. The companion said this was a sign from Allah SWT. The prophet PBUH said, "No, do not say that." In addition, he said "The sun and the moon are signs from Allah SWT and they do not eclipse because of the death or birth of any human." If he wanted glory or power, he would have said yes.

As the holy Quran is not written by the prophet Mohammed PBUH, what is the proof that it was revealed by Almighty God? The answer to this question is given in the next section.

6.4 What is the proof that the holy Quran was revealed by Almighty God?

History witnesses that the holy Quran correctly predicted many future events. Throughout history, there was no human who could predict his own future or the future of others. All people who try to predict the future base their prediction on probability and expectation. Therefore, their prediction is never completely correct. However, all predictions in the holy Quran were always correct.

The holy Quran predicted victory for Muslims at the time when they were very weak and it was impossible for anyone to see such a victory. To migrate from Mecca to Al-Medina, the prophet PBUH and his companions had left all their wealth behind in Mecca. Muslims started their life in Al-Medina in very poor circumstances and a weak situation. They could not even find enough food to survive. At the same time, they had to fight against three kinds of enemies: the nonbelievers of Quraysh, who attacked them from outside Al-Medina; the Jews, who attacked them from inside Al-Medina; and the hypocrites amongst themselves. Thus, the Muslims were waiting for numerous attacks from their enemies, and they did not have enough power to protect themselves. During all these troubles, the holy Quran predicted victory for the Muslims.

[58:21] *Allah has written down: I will most certainly prevail, I and My messengers; surely Allah is Strong, Mighty.*

[61:8] *They desire to put out the light of Allah with their mouths but Allah will perfect His light, though the unbelievers may be averse.*

[61:9] *He it is Who sent His messenger with the guidance and the true religion, that He may make it overcome the religions, all of them, though the polytheists may be averse.*

After the revelation of these verses, Muslims started to gain victories over the tribe of Quraysh in the Arabian Peninsula and Jews in Al-Medina. The prophet PBUH and a small number of Muslims were able to build the Islamic empire and defeat the Romans and Persians, the two biggest empires at that time. It is not possible to assume that such a prediction in these circumstances could have been made by a human. Only Almighty God, who knew what had happened and what would happen, could have made such a prediction.

Another correct prediction by the holy Quran is the victory of the Roman Empire over the Persian Empire, at the time when the Persians were leading a very tough battle. The Romans were Christians, while the Persians were worshippers of fire. Muslims were (spiritually) on the side of the Romans because they were people of the Book and Christendom is one of the heavenly religions, whereas the nonbelievers of Quraysh were on the side of the Persians, as they had a kind of idol worship religion similar to theirs.

At the beginning of the battle, the Persians had an advantage over the Romans. They destroyed the churches, killed more than 100,000 innocent Christians, built temples to worship fire and forced people to worship the sun and fire. The nonbelievers of Quraysh were very happy with this victory and said to the Muslims, "Our brothers defeated your brothers, so we will defeat you too." The Muslims were very weak at that time, similar to the Romans. In these circumstances and during these events, the holy Quran predicted the victory of the Romans a few years later.

[30:2-4] *The Roman Empire has been defeated; In a land close by; but they, (even) after (this) defeat of theirs, will soon be victorious; Within a few years. With Allah is the Decision, in the past and in the Future: on that Day shall the Believers rejoice.*

Although the Roman Empire was very weak at that time, the holy Quran predicted its victory. And indeed, after a few years, the Romans were able to rebuild their army and defeated the Persians in six consecutive wars.

Many other events were predicted correctly by the holy Quran. The conquest of Mecca and the victory of the prophet PBUH and his companions over the nonbelievers of Mecca were predicted by the holy Quran at the time when no military expert could predict their occurrence.

[48:27] *Certainly Allah had shown to His messenger the vision with truth: you shall most certainly enter the Sacred Mosque, if Allah pleases, in security, (some) having their heads shaved and (others) having their hair cut, you shall not fear, but He knows what you do not know, so He brought about a near victory before that.*

The holy Quran also predicted the future outcome of Abu Lahab, the uncle of the prophet and one of the biggest enemies of the Islam. It predicted that Abu Lahab would die as a non-Muslim and that he would keep rejecting the Islamic message, therefore deserving to go to hell. The following verses were revealed ten years before Abu Lahab's death.

[111:1-3] *Perdition overtake both hands of Abu Lahab, and he will perish. His wealth and what he earns will not avail him. He shall soon burn in fire that flames.*

The holy Quran also predicted numerous scientific facts which were discovered during the last century. Muslim scholars identified up to 100 scientific facts that were mentioned in the holy Quran more than 1,400 years ago. We mention a few of them in this book, *Part I: Faith issues*. However, we will present more than 50 scientific facts in detail in *Part II: Scientific issues*, Insha'Allah.

The holy Quran mentioned the big-bang theory, which is a scientific fact and universally accepted by scientists.

[21:30] *Have not those who disbelieve known that the heavens and the Earth were joined together as one united piece, then We parted them? And We have made from water every living thing. Will they not then believe?*

The holy Quran mentioned the scientific fact that the universe is expanding and that it continues to expand.

[51:47] *With power did We construct the heaven. Verily, We are Able to extend the vastness of space thereof.*

The holy Quran mentioned that at the time when earth was created, the succession of night and day was very fast. Nowadays, this is a scientific fact.

[7:54] *Indeed your Lord is Allah, Who created the heavens and the Earth in Six Days, and then He Istawâ (rose over) the Throne (really in a manner that suits His Majesty). He brings the night as a cover over the day, seeking it rapidly.*

Modern scientists have discovered that water originally came from volcanoes, which are generated from earth. This scientific fact is mentioned in the holy Quran by indicating that water was brought from earth.

[79:30-31] *And after that He spread the Earth; And brought forth there from its water and its pasture.*

The spherical shape of the earth was recently discovered by modern science. However, it is mentioned in the holy Quran in the following verse:

[39:5] *He created the heavens and the earth in true (proportions): He makes the Night overlap (coil) the Day, and the Day overlap (coil) the Night.*

The night overlaps or coils the day, and vice versa. This can only happen if the earth is spherical.

If any person would try to guess all these scientific facts, 50 or more, and predict future events as the holy Quran did 1,400 years ago, the probability of guessing them correctly is quasi-zero. The theory of probability tells us that the probability of guessing an event, which has only two options: yes or no, correctly is 0.5 or 50%. Furthermore, it tells us that the probability of predicting two events correctly, each having two options, is 0.5×0.5 = 0.25 or 25%.

If an event has n options, its probability is $1/n$ and the probability for two such events is $1/n \times 1/n$. For example, predicting victory of the Romans over the Persians had two options and its probability was 0.5 or 50%. The prediction of the movement of the universe had three options – expansion, contraction or remaining the same – and its probability was 1/3 = 0.333 or 33%. The probability to predict that the shape of the earth is spherical was 1/9 = 0.111

or 11% as there are nine options for 3D shapes: sphere, torus, cylinder, cone, cube, cuboid, triangular pyramid, square pyramid and prism.

Thus, if we assume that the average probability of all events is 0.25, the probability for guessing 50 events of scientific facts correctly will be equal to $0.25^{50} = 7.89 \times 10^{-31}$. This means that it is impossible that the holy Quran was written by a human or that it was based on humans' predictions. The exact figure of each event and the probability of guessing all of them will be discussed in detail in *Part II: Scientific issues*, Insha'Allah.

The above concept is illustrated in logic flowchart 50. The statement saying that the holy Quran predicted many future events correctly and mentioned many scientific facts correctly is a fact. Furthermore, the statement saying that all predicted events and scientific facts cannot be correct by chance (through the theory of probability as demonstrated above) is also a fact. Therefore, the holy Quran cannot have been written by a human and should be the words of Almighty God. The statement saying that all predicted events and scientific facts can be correct by chance is against the Law of Identity and not logical.

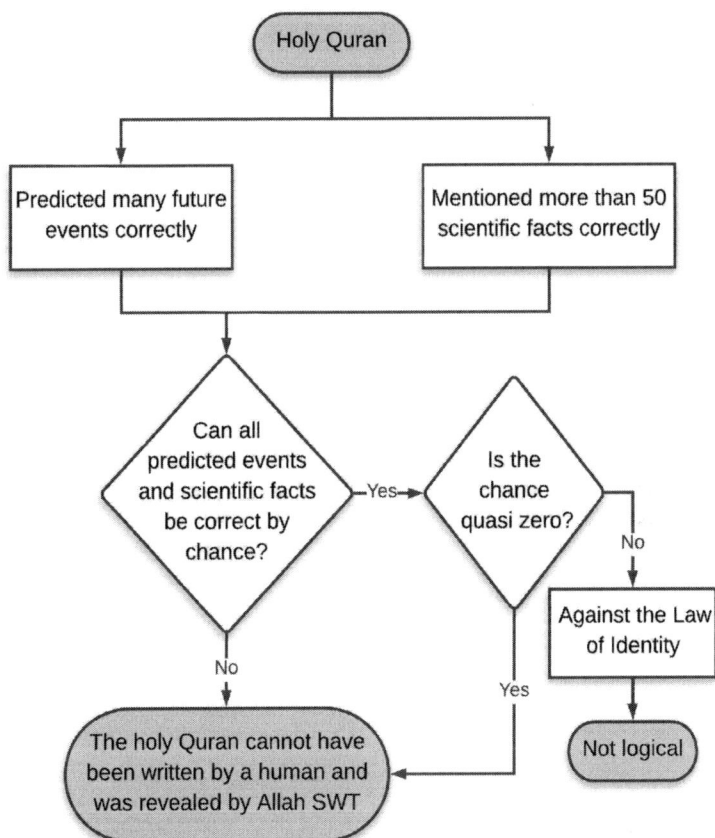

Logic flowchart 50: The holy Quran - Example 5

7 The Islam

7.1 Why Islam as a religion?

As explained in a previous chapter, all heavenly religions are in fact one religion. All prophets from the generation of Ibrahim PBUH, and even before, have the same message: "There is only one god, worship only one god and do not associate anyone else with Almighty God, who is perfect and complete." This message has never changed but, throughout history, people have disobeyed and have failed to follow the original message. This is why Almighty God has sent prophet after prophet to the disobedient people who made changes in the religion of Almighty God.

In fact, one condition for believing in the Islam is to believe in all prophets sent by Almighty God, including Moses PBUH, Jesus PBUH and Mohammed PBUH. If a Muslim does not believe in all prophets, his belief is not complete. All prophets can be regarded as a chain and the prophet Mohammed PBUH is the last link in this chain. Similarly, a Muslim should believe in all holy books revealed by Allah SWT, including the holy Quran, the original Bible and the original Torah (first testament).

Allah SWT mentions in the holy Quran that all religions from Him are in fact one religion, the Islam, which in the Arabic language means 'submit to Allah SWT and worship only Him.' All the prophets have been sent with the same religion – the message of the Islam.

[3:19] *Surely the (true) religion with Allah is Islam.*

As mentioned in the previous chapter, the original message of the Islam sent by prophets Jesus PBUH and Moses PBUH in the holy books, the original Bible and the original Torah, has been changed, altered and corrupted by Jews and Christians throughout history.

[5:13] *And because of their breaking their covenant, We have cursed them and made hard their hearts. They change words from their context and forget a part of that whereof they were admonished.*

The Christians have changed the original message of the Islam by associating a son (partner) with Almighty God.

[19:88-93] *And they say: The Beneficent Allah has taken (to Himself) a son. Certainly you have made a disastrous thing. The heavens may almost be rent thereat, and the earth cleave asunder, and the mountains fall down in pieces. That they ascribe a son to the Beneficent Allah. And it is not worthy of the Beneficent Allah that He should take (to Himself) a son. There is no one in the heavens and the earth but will come to the Beneficent Allah as a servant.*

However, Jesus PBUH never said to his people that he was god. To the contrary, like all other prophets, he delivered to them the message of the Islam: "There is only one absolute complete perfect Almighty God."

[5:116] *And when Allah will say: O Jesus, son of Mary! did you say to men, Take me and my mother for two gods besides Allah he will say: Glory be to Thee, it did not befit me that I should say what I had no right to (say); if I had said it, Thou wouldst indeed have known it; Thou knowest what is in my mind, and I do not know what is in Thy mind, surely Thou art the great Knower of the unseen things.*

The Jews have changed the original message of the Islam by associating wrong characteristics with Almighty God, which describe Him as an incomplete and imperfect god. They have made many changes and modifications in the original Torah which indicate the association of sleepiness, tiredness, unjustness, unfairness and lack of wisdom with Almighty God. The Jews further described Almighty God as ungenerous.

[5:64] *And the Jews say: The hand of Allah is tied up! Their hands shall be shackled and they shall be cursed for what they say. Nay, both His hands are spread out, He expends as He pleases; and what has been revealed to you from your Lord will certainly make many of them increase in inordinacy and unbelief; and We have put enmity and hatred amongst them till the day of resurrection; whenever they kindle a fire for war Allah puts it out, and they strive to make mischief in the land; and Allah does not love the mischief-makers.*

The corrupted Torah insulted prophets and the Jews killed many of them. Even when Jesus PBUH was sent to them to correct their wrong behaviours and the corrupted Torah, they insulted his mother, attacked him and tried to kill him. By insulting and killing prophets, the Jews indirectly said that the choice of prophets by Almighty God was not correct and they challenged His wisdom and perfection.

[4:155] *Therefore, for their breaking their covenant and their disbelief in the communications of Allah and their killing the prophets wrongfully and their saying: Our hearts are covered; nay! Allah set a seal upon them owing to their unbelief, so they shall not believe except a few.*

Logic flowchart 51 demonstrates the concept of the original message of Islam. In principle, all heavenly religions are the same and have the same message. However, Jews have changed the original message by describing Almighty God as incomplete and associating many wrong characteristics with Him. The Christians have also changed the original message by associating a son (partner) with Almighty God. Islam then came to return people to the original message and correct the flawed concepts introduced by Jews and Christians throughout history.

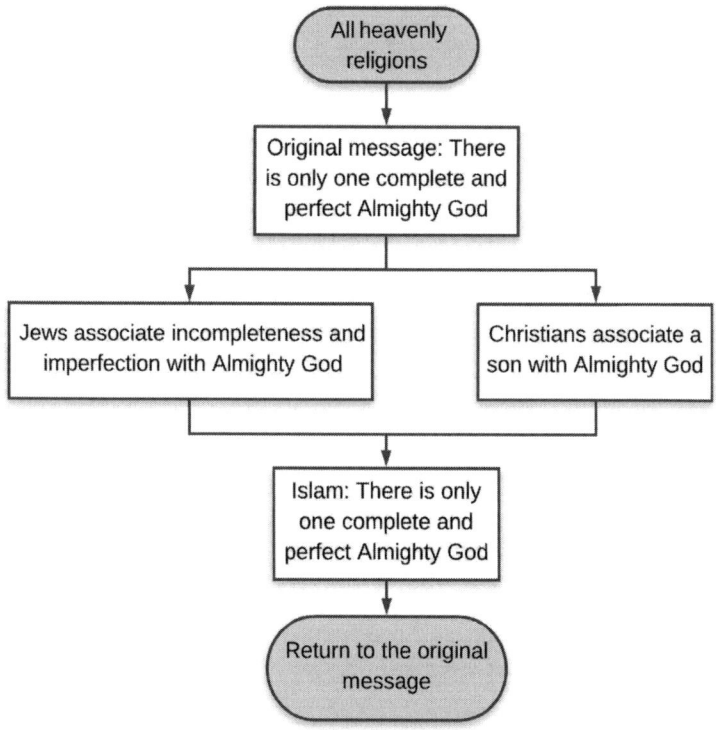

Logic flowchart 51: The Islam - Example 1

Allah SWT asks the people of the Book, i.e. the Jews and Christians, to agree on only one common word, that is, to worship only Him and to not associate any partner with Him.

[3:64] *Say: O People of the Scripture! Come to an agreement between us and you: that we shall worship none but Allah, and that we shall ascribe no partner unto Him, and that none of us shall take others for lords beside Allah. And if they turn away, then say: Bear witness that we are they who have surrendered (unto Him).*

As Islam is the last heavenly religion, why was the prophet Mohammed PBUH chosen to deliver this final message? What were the special characteristics of the prophet Mohammed PBUH to make him a messenger of Almighty God? Are these characteristics the same as for all other prophets before him? Were the characteristics of the prophet Mohammed PBUH the same before and after the revelation? The answers to these questions are provided in the next section.

7.2 Why was Mohammed PBUH chosen to be prophet?

Sending messengers by Almighty God to humans is essential to guide them and show them the right path. Since thousands of years, humans have been looking for the truth and trying to understand the secrets of life. They have been trying to find answers to many questions about the start and the end of life, the purpose of life, the purpose of good and evil, and death. Although science and technology have advanced in the past and at present, they do not provide answers to these questions. Therefore, we need directions from the creator, Almighty God, to show us the right way.

Therefore, Almighty God has sent many messengers and the last messenger was the prophet Mohammed PBUH. He, the prophet of Islam, recognised all messengers sent by Allah SWT before him. Therefore, if his message was proven, the message of all prophets before him were automatically proven.

A messenger of Almighty God or a prophet should have a special noble character that no one else has. Allah SWT will choose the best person amongst humans to reveal His message to them. This condition is applicable to all prophets sent to humanity throughout history, including Moses PBUH and Jesus PBUH. If the character of this person is exceptionally high, he should be honest and we have to believe him. Furthermore, if his message has extraordinary information that a normal human being cannot have, then again people have to believe him.

Looking back at history, we can see without any doubt that the prophet Mohammed PBUH was of very high, noble character, before and after the revelation from Allah SWT. The prophet PBUH was born in Mecca and received the revelation from Allah SWT when he was 40 years old. During these 40 years, he was known amongst his people and his tribe as the most honest and truthful person. His tribe agreed, with no exception, on his honesty and truthfulness.

Five years before the revelation of the message of Islam, when the tribe of Quraysh (the tribe of the prophet in Mecca) wanted to rebuild the house of Allah (Kaaba), they had a dispute about who would lay the last piece of stone. This dispute continued for four or five days, until they agreed to accept the judgement of the first person who entered the Kaaba. The next day, the first person entering the Kaaba was the prophet Mohammed PBUH, so they all agreed and said, "He is the most honest and trustworthy person. We accept his judgement."

When the revelation started and the angel Gabriel came to the prophet PBUH for the first time, he went to his wife, Khadijah, may Allah SWT be pleased with her, and he was very scared. She said to him, "Allah SWT will never disappoint you because you do good to your family, to your guests, and to people in need." And when the tribe of Quraysh had gathered on the mountain, the prophet told them, "If I tell you that behind this mountain are horses, would you believe me?" They replied, "Sure, we believe you; you never lie."

Three years after establishing the Islamic state in Al-Medina, the prophet Mohammed PBUH sent a message to the Hercules roman king to invite him to Islam. The king asked to bring a man from the prophet tribe who is the closest to the prophet PBUH and has the best knowledge of him. The soldiers brought Abou-Sofian, who was a nonbeliever at that time. The king asked Abou-Sofian, "Has Mohammed ever lied." Abou-Sofian replied, "No, he has never lied." The king said, "If he never lied to people, how can he lie to God?"

The prophet Mohammed PBUH suffered a lot from his folk. During his 13-year stay in Mecca after revelation, his tribe did all possible evils to him in order to prevent him from delivering his message. The nonbelievers of Quraysh put dirt on his way and threw stones at him and his followers. They also applied sanctions so food would not reach him or his followers for three years. The sanctions were so severe; they ate leaves off trees as nothing else was available. Despite the torture and wrongdoing by the nonbelievers, the prophet PBUH stood by his message and continued to enjoy good and forbid evil. The nonbelievers decided to kill him, so he emigrated from Mecca to Al-Medina, where he started the Islamic empire.

After the immigration of the prophet PBUH to Al-Medina, the nonbelievers of Mecca started to organised wars to attack Al-Medina and destroy the Islam. And after ten years in Al-Medina, the prophet returned to Mecca with a big army and he had a great victory over the nonbelievers of his tribe Quraysh. When he entered Mecca, the prophet PBUH asked the nonbelievers, "What do you think I will do with you?" They answered, "You are a generous brother and your father was a generous brother." The prophet PBUH said to them, "Go, you are free."

This historic story just let us see how noble and great the character of the prophet was. A normal human would never be able to do that. This is something that has never been seen before or after the prophet PBUH. It is clearly documented in history, and no one can deny that it happened.

Before the revelation, the prophet was a rich man as he was working in his family trade business. His wife Khadijah, may Allah SWT be pleased with her, was a very rich woman and together, they could live a wealthy life. But they spent all their wealth to spread the message of Islam and preferred to live a poor life.

The prophet Mohammed PBUH was an example of humbleness who listened to everyone. After the revelation, the nonbelievers of Quraysh offered him wealth and a kingdom in order to stop his message. They came to him and said, "If you want wealth, we will gather money from all tribes and give it to you. And if you want a kingdom, we will make you king." The prophet PBUH refused all these offers and replied, "If they bring the sun to my right side and the moon to my left side, I will never stop delivering the message of Islam until Allah SWT delivers it to all mankind."

Allah SWT described the character of the prophet Mohammed PBUH to be of exalted standard.

[68:4] *And thou (standest) on an exalted standard of character.*

Logic flowchart 52 illustrates that, as history witnessed that the prophet Mohammed PBUH was of high, noble character, he was the most trustful human to deliver the message of Allah SWT.

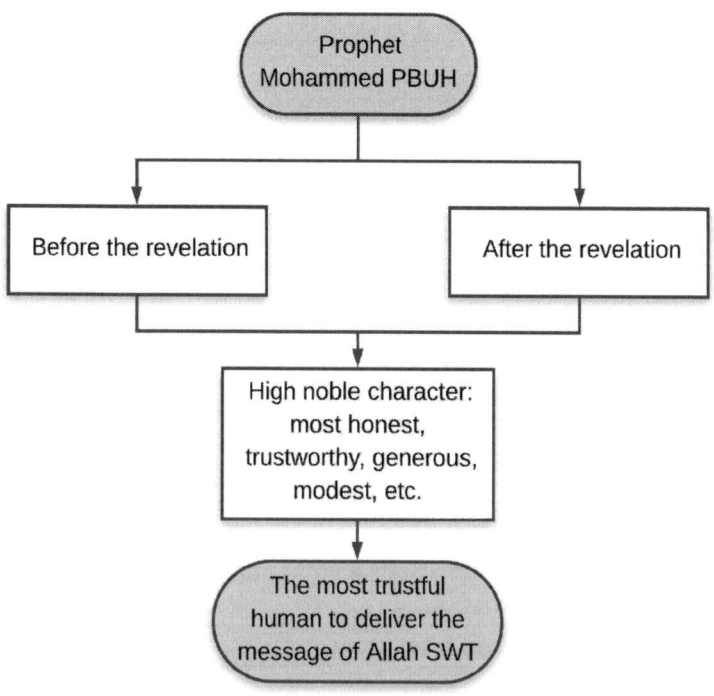

Logic flowchart 52: The Islam - Example 2

The next question in this chapter relates to the reason why the prophet Mohammed PBUH was the last messenger of Almighty God. Why did Almighty God not send more messengers after Mohammed PBUH? Is there a need for more messengers and more holy scriptures? We answer these questions in the next section.

7.3 Why was prophet Mohammed PBUH the last messenger of Almighty God?

As mentioned earlier, all prophets came with the same message of monotheism, which is also the message of Islam. However, throughout history, people have changed and modified the original message to their own benefit.

[2:75] *Have ye any hope that they will be true to you when a party of them used to listen to the word of Allah, then used to change it, after they had understood it, knowingly?*

Every prophet came to correct the changes made by people in the monotheism concept and in the holy scriptures. Allah SWT promised that the last scripture, the holy Quran, would never be corrupted by people and would forever be protected by Himself against any change or corruption.

[15:9] *Surely We have revealed the Reminder (the Quran) and We will most surely be its guardian.*

It is a fact that no single letter has ever been changed in the holy Quran since it was revealed more than 1,400 years ago. Consequently, the original message of Islam and monotheism will remain unchanged on earth until the day of judgement. Thus, by revealing the holy Quran, the religion of Allah SWT and His message to humanity are complete.

[5:3] *This day have I perfected for you your religion and completed My favor on you and chosen for you Islam as a religion.*

Therefore, the prophet Mohammed PBUH is the last prophet and there is no need for more prophets.

[33:40] *Muhammad is not the father of any of your men, but he is the messenger of Allah and the Last of the prophets; and Allah is cognizant of all things.*

The above concept is illustrated in logic flowchart 53. The statement saying that the holy Quran, which contains the message of Islam (monotheism), has not been changed since it was revealed to prophet Mohammed PBUH, is a fact. Therefore, there is no need for more prophets and it is logical that prophet Mohammed PBUH is the last prophet. The statement saying that the holy Quran has been changed in the last 1,400 years is against the Law of Identity.

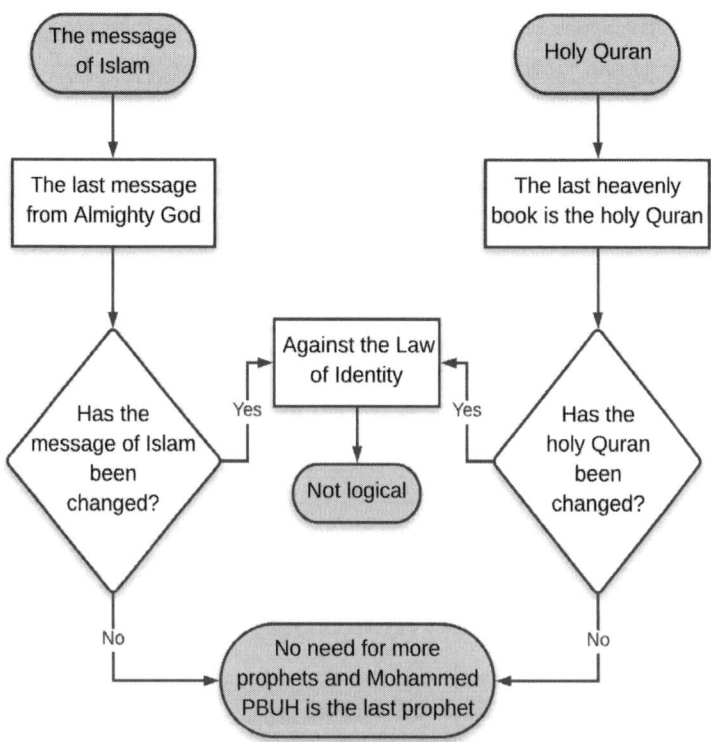

Logic flowchart 53: The Islam - Example 3

The original Bible sates that Jesus PBUH delivered the message that a last prophet would be sent by Allah SWT. The name of the last prophet was mentioned in the original Bible as Ahmed, which is another name for the prophet Mohammed PBUH.

[61:6] And remember, Jesus, the son of Mary, said: "O Children of Israel! I am the messenger of Allah (sent) to you, confirming the Law (which came) before me, and giving Glad Tidings of a messenger to come after me, whose name shall be Ahmad." But when he came to them with Clear Signs, they said, "this is evident sorcery!"

The prophet Mohammed PBUH is at the end of the chain of prophets. He is completing the religion of Allah SWT and His message to humanity.

Narrated by Jabir bin Abdullah: The prophet said, "My similitude in comparison with the other prophets is that of a man who has built a house completely and excellently except for a place of one brick. When the people enter the house, they admire its beauty and say: 'But for the place of this brick (how splendid the house will be)!" (Sahih Bukhari, Book #56, Hadith #734)

The last question in this chapter is related to an Islamic practice, the Tawaf, i.e. the action of revolving around the house of Allah SWT in Mecca. Some people see this action as a kind of worshipping stones or idols. Does this action indeed violate the monotheism principle? What is the reason for performing the Tawaf? Is there a symbolic reason for doing it? In the next section, the answers to these questions will be given.

7.4 Is the Tawaf a sort of worshipping stone?

The Tawaf means revolving around the house of Allah SWT (Kaaba) in Mecca during pilgrimage and regular visits. This action is considered as worshipping Almighty God. The prophet PBUH said that it is similar to praying, with the exception that talking to others is allowed during Tawaf. The house of Allah SWT is built of stone, so what is the logical reason for this Tawaf?

We observe in the creations around us, in material sciences and astronomy, that the small objects revolve around the big objects. The electron revolves around the nucleus of an atom. The moon revolves around the earth, and the earth revolves around the sun. The sun revolves around the centre of the galaxy, and the galaxy revolves around a bigger galaxy, until we reach the biggest and greatest, that is, Almighty God. Everything in the universe is moving, except Allah SWT, who is independent of motion and time as He is above all His creations.

Revolving around the Kaaba in Mecca is therefore a symbolic sort of praying and submitting to Almighty God. We are all on earth and we revolve around the sun and the galaxies, as an act of worship, without our input. We are obliged to do so; we do not have a choice. However, revolving around the house of Allah in Mecca is our own choice and therefore it is a kind of prayer and forms a part of the test, i.e. obey or disobey Almighty God. This house in Mecca is the first house built on earth to worship Allah SWT. Therefore, revolving around it is a symbolic action to worship Allah SWT.

A comparison between objects revolving around each other and Muslims revolving around Kaaba is illustrated in logic flowchart 54. The statement saying that small objects do not choose to revolve around big objects is a fact. Similarly, the statement saying that Muslims choose to revolve around the Kaaba is also a fact. Therefore, the opposite statements are against the Law of Identity. The objects are forced to obey and worship Allah SWT, while Muslims choose to obey and worship Allah SWT.

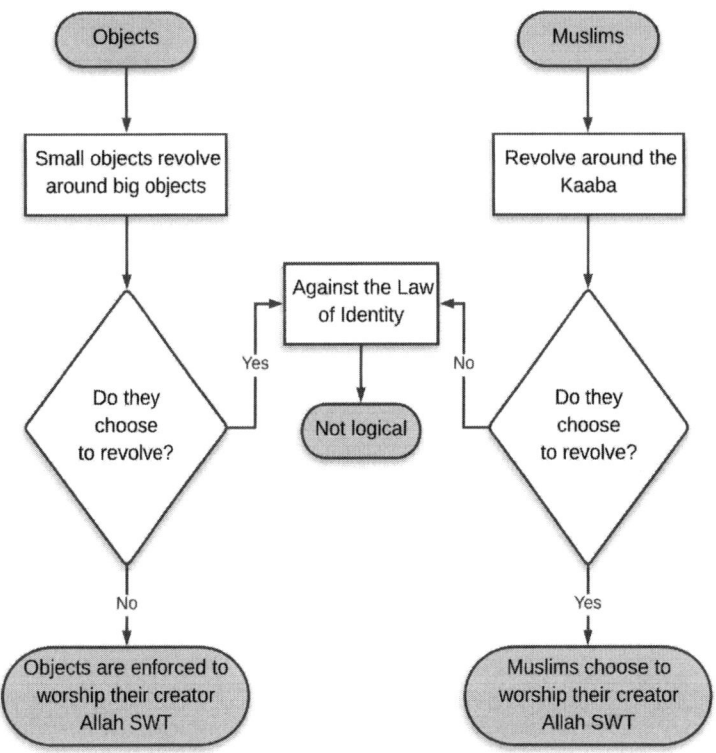

Logic flowchart 54: The Tawaf - Example 1

Muslims revolve around the Kaaba seven times. The number seven also has a symbolic meaning related to creations. According to the holy Quran, the number of heavens is seven. The number of colours in the light spectrum is seven. Babies born before seven months face a high risk of dying. The week consists of seven days, for all people on earth. Therefore, for the Tawaf, the number seven also has a symbolic meaning.

The first ever pilgrimage was done by the prophet Ibrahim PBUH. He was called the father of prophets. All prophets, including Mohammed PBUH, Jesus PBUH and Moses PBUH, came from his generation. Muslims perform pilgrimage as part of Islamic obligation, to repeat exactly what the prophet Ibrahim PBUH did. This includes leaving their homes, going to Mecca, going to the mountain Arafat, throwing stones at the devil and doing the Tawaf around the Kaaba. This way, they repeat what the prophet Ibrahim PBUH did to obey and worship Allah SWT.

The prophet Ibrahim PBUH and his son Ismail PBUH built the Kaaba.

[2:127] *And when Ibrahim and Ismail raised the foundations of the House: Our Lord! accept from us; surely Thou art the Hearing, the Knowing.*

Allah SWT asked Ibrahim PBUH to build the Kaaba and showed him its place.

[22:26] *And when We assigned to Ibrahim the place of the House, saying: Do not associate with Me aught, and purify My House for those who make the circuit and stand to pray and bow and prostrate themselves.*

And Allah SWT asked Ibrahim PBUH to call people to perform the pilgrimage.

[22:27] *And proclaim amongst men the Pilgrimage: they will come to you on foot and on every lean camel, coming from every remote path.*

The pilgrimage is therefore a response to the call of the prophet Ibrahim PBUH, a symbolic action required by every Muslim to show his obedience and his readiness to do what Allah SWT asked Ibrahim PBUH to do. The pilgrimage is an Islamic pillar that contains many different types of worship, such as praying in the Kaaba mosque, spending money in the sake of Allah SWT, remembering Allah SWT and, in some specific cases, fasting.

The pilgrimage can also be seen as a symbolic trip to Allah SWT in this worldly life. The place of pilgrimage, Mecca, is chosen by Allah SWT as the centre of His messages to Ibrahim PBUH and Mohammed PBUH. In the pilgrimage, people from all over the world come in large numbers to the same place at the same time, wearing the same clothes and mentioning the name of Almighty

God in the same way. This reminds us of the day of resurrection when all people will be forced to rise from the dead and come to Allah SWT.

[36:51] *And the trumpet shall be blown, when lo! from their graves they shall hasten on to their Lord.*

It is therefore a symbolic picture of what will happen on the day of judgement. For Muslims, the pilgrimage is required only once in a lifetime provided they are physically and financially capable.

Finally, the Kaaba in Mecca can also be regarded as a symbol for unity of Muslims around the world. When Muslims pray, which they do five times a day, they have to face the Kaaba. Therefore, the Kaaba is a symbol for worshipping Almighty God on earth and for the unity of Muslims.

About the author

Prof. Dr. Magd Abdel Wahab is a full-time Professor of Applied Mechanics in the Faculty of Engineering and Architecture at Ghent University, Belgium and an Associate Imam at Badr mosque in Ledeberg, Ghent, Belgium. He received Bachelor of Science and Master of Science degrees in Civil Engineering from the Cairo University. Prof. Wahab completed his Doctor of Philosophy, PhD, degree in 1995 at KU Leuven, Belgium. He was further awarded the degree of Doctor of Science, DSc, by the University of Surrey, UK, in 2008. He has published more than 400 scientific papers, and has written and edited more than 19 books and proceedings in the field of engineering. Beside his interest in engineering, Prof. Wahab has a strong interest in research in Islamic religion. During the last 15 years, he has served as an Associate Imam, and has delivered Friday ceremony speeches and Islamic talks in several mosques in the UK and Belgium. This book, *Logic and Islam*, summarises his experiences and provides logical answers to questions related to Almighty God, creations and Islam.